C-4896   CAREER EXAMINATION SERIES

This is your
PASSBOOK for...

Heating and Air Conditioning Maintainer

Test Preparation Study Guide
Questions & Answers

NATIONAL LEARNING CORPORATION®

COPYRIGHT NOTICE

This book is SOLELY intended for, is sold ONLY to, and its use is RESTRICTED to individual, bona fide applicants or candidates who qualify by virtue of having seriously filed applications for appropriate license, certificate, professional and/or promotional advancement, higher school matriculation, scholarship, or other legitimate requirements of education and/or governmental authorities.

This book is NOT intended for use, class instruction, tutoring, training, duplication, copying, reprinting, excerption, or adaptation, etc., by:

1) Other publishers
2) Proprietors and/or Instructors of "Coaching" and/or Preparatory Courses
3) Personnel and/or Training Divisions of commercial, industrial, and governmental organizations
4) Schools, colleges, or universities and/or their departments and staffs, including teachers and other personnel
5) Testing Agencies or Bureaus
6) Study groups which seek by the purchase of a single volume to copy and/or duplicate and/or adapt this material for use by the group as a whole without having purchased individual volumes for each of the members of the group
7) Et al.

Such persons would be in violation of appropriate Federal and State statutes.

PROVISION OF LICENSING AGREEMENTS – Recognized educational, commercial, industrial, and governmental institutions and organizations, and others legitimately engaged in educational pursuits, including training, testing, and measurement activities, may address request for a licensing agreement to the copyright owners, who will determine whether, and under what conditions, including fees and charges, the materials in this book may be used them. In other words, a licensing facility exists for the legitimate use of the material in this book on other than an individual basis. However, it is asseverated and affirmed here that the material in this book CANNOT be used without the receipt of the express permission of such a licensing agreement from the Publishers. Inquiries re licensing should be addressed to the company, attention rights and permissions department.

All rights reserved, including the right of reproduction in whole or in part, in any form or by any means, electronic or mechanical, including photocopying, recording, or by any information storage and retrieval system, without permission in writing from the Publisher.

Copyright © 2024 by

National Learning Corporation

212 Michael Drive, Syosset, NY 11791
(516) 921-8888 • www.passbooks.com
E-mail: info@passbooks.com

PASSBOOK® SERIES

THE *PASSBOOK® SERIES* has been created to prepare applicants and candidates for the ultimate academic battlefield – the examination room.

At some time in our lives, each and every one of us may be required to take an examination – for validation, matriculation, admission, qualification, registration, certification, or licensure.

Based on the assumption that every applicant or candidate has met the basic formal educational standards, has taken the required number of courses, and read the necessary texts, the *PASSBOOK® SERIES* furnishes the one special preparation which may assure passing with confidence, instead of failing with insecurity. Examination questions – together with answers – are furnished as the basic vehicle for study so that the mysteries of the examination and its compounding difficulties may be eliminated or diminished by a sure method.

This book is meant to help you pass your examination provided that you qualify and are serious in your objective.

The entire field is reviewed through the huge store of content information which is succinctly presented through a provocative and challenging approach – the question-and-answer method.

A climate of success is established by furnishing the correct answers at the end of each test.

You soon learn to recognize types of questions, forms of questions, and patterns of questioning. You may even begin to anticipate expected outcomes.

You perceive that many questions are repeated or adapted so that you can gain acute insights, which may enable you to score many sure points.

You learn how to confront new questions, or types of questions, and to attack them confidently and work out the correct answers.

You note objectives and emphases, and recognize pitfalls and dangers, so that you may make positive educational adjustments.

Moreover, you are kept fully informed in relation to new concepts, methods, practices, and directions in the field.

You discover that you are actually taking the examination all the time: you are preparing for the examination by "taking" an examination, not by reading extraneous and/or supererogatory textbooks.

In short, this PASSBOOK®, used directedly, should be an important factor in helping you to pass your test.

HEATING AND AIR CONDITIONING MAINTAINER

JOB DESCRIPTION:

Heating and Air Conditioning Maintainers, under supervision, maintain, install, inspect, test, alter, and repair heating and air conditioning systems and equipment of City Transit structures, such as shops, stations, and buildings. They work on air conditioners and components, such as compressors, condensers, evaporators, fans, motors, electrical and electronic controls and valves. They work on boilers, furnaces and components, such as boiler sections, heaters, radiators, piping, pumps, motors, and electrical and electronic controls and valves. They solder and braze, keep records, write reports, and perform related work.

THE TEST;

The qualifying multiple choice test may include questions on basic electrical theory; electrical, mechanical, pneumatic and hydraulic devices and components related to the heating and air conditioning trade; proper selection and use of tools, instruments and materials; safe, proper and efficient work practices; reading and interpreting blueprints and drawings; performing job-related calculations; keeping records and other related areas.

The competitive practical skills test may include tasks related to the installation, testing, maintenance, and repair of electrical, electronic, mechanical, and electromechanical components and systems related to the heating and air conditioning trade, including the selection and use of appropriate tools, materials, and measuring devices; related mechanical work; reading and interpreting technical drawings; shop math; safe work practices and procedures; and other related areas.

HOW TO TAKE A TEST

I. YOU MUST PASS AN EXAMINATION

A. *WHAT EVERY CANDIDATE SHOULD KNOW*

Examination applicants often ask us for help in preparing for the written test. What can I study in advance? What kinds of questions will be asked? How will the test be given? How will the papers be graded?

As an applicant for a civil service examination, you may be wondering about some of these things. Our purpose here is to suggest effective methods of advance study and to describe civil service examinations.

Your chances for success on this examination can be increased if you know how to prepare. Those "pre-examination jitters" can be reduced if you know what to expect. You can even experience an adventure in good citizenship if you know why civil service exams are given.

B. *WHY ARE CIVIL SERVICE EXAMINATIONS GIVEN?*

Civil service examinations are important to you in two ways. As a citizen, you want public jobs filled by employees who know how to do their work. As a job seeker, you want a fair chance to compete for that job on an equal footing with other candidates. The best-known means of accomplishing this two-fold goal is the competitive examination.

Exams are widely publicized throughout the nation. They may be administered for jobs in federal, state, city, municipal, town or village governments or agencies.

Any citizen may apply, with some limitations, such as the age or residence of applicants. Your experience and education may be reviewed to see whether you meet the requirements for the particular examination. When these requirements exist, they are reasonable and applied consistently to all applicants. Thus, a competitive examination may cause you some uneasiness now, but it is your privilege and safeguard.

C. *HOW ARE CIVIL SERVICE EXAMS DEVELOPED?*

Examinations are carefully written by trained technicians who are specialists in the field known as "psychological measurement," in consultation with recognized authorities in the field of work that the test will cover. These experts recommend the subject matter areas or skills to be tested; only those knowledges or skills important to your success on the job are included. The most reliable books and source materials available are used as references. Together, the experts and technicians judge the difficulty level of the questions.

Test technicians know how to phrase questions so that the problem is clearly stated. Their ethics do not permit "trick" or "catch" questions. Questions may have been tried out on sample groups, or subjected to statistical analysis, to determine their usefulness.

Written tests are often used in combination with performance tests, ratings of training and experience, and oral interviews. All of these measures combine to form the best-known means of finding the right person for the right job.

II. HOW TO PASS THE WRITTEN TEST

A. NATURE OF THE EXAMINATION

To prepare intelligently for civil service examinations, you should know how they differ from school examinations you have taken. In school you were assigned certain definite pages to read or subjects to cover. The examination questions were quite detailed and usually emphasized memory. Civil service exams, on the other hand, try to discover your present ability to perform the duties of a position, plus your potentiality to learn these duties. In other words, a civil service exam attempts to predict how successful you will be. Questions cover such a broad area that they cannot be as minute and detailed as school exam questions.

In the public service similar kinds of work, or positions, are grouped together in one "class." This process is known as *position-classification*. All the positions in a class are paid according to the salary range for that class. One class title covers all of these positions, and they are all tested by the same examination.

B. FOUR BASIC STEPS

1) Study the announcement

How, then, can you know what subjects to study? Our best answer is: "Learn as much as possible about the class of positions for which you've applied." The exam will test the knowledge, skills and abilities needed to do the work.

Your most valuable source of information about the position you want is the official exam announcement. This announcement lists the training and experience qualifications. Check these standards and apply only if you come reasonably close to meeting them.

The brief description of the position in the examination announcement offers some clues to the subjects which will be tested. Think about the job itself. Review the duties in your mind. Can you perform them, or are there some in which you are rusty? Fill in the blank spots in your preparation.

Many jurisdictions preview the written test in the exam announcement by including a section called "Knowledge and Abilities Required," "Scope of the Examination," or some similar heading. Here you will find out specifically what fields will be tested.

2) Review your own background

Once you learn in general what the position is all about, and what you need to know to do the work, ask yourself which subjects you already know fairly well and which need improvement. You may wonder whether to concentrate on improving your strong areas or on building some background in your fields of weakness. When the announcement has specified "some knowledge" or "considerable knowledge," or has used adjectives like "beginning principles of…" or "advanced … methods," you can get a clue as to the number and difficulty of questions to be asked in any given field. More questions, and hence broader coverage, would be included for those subjects which are more important in the work. Now weigh your strengths and weaknesses against the job requirements and prepare accordingly.

3) Determine the level of the position

Another way to tell how intensively you should prepare is to understand the level of the job for which you are applying. Is it the entering level? In other words, is this the position in which beginners in a field of work are hired? Or is it an intermediate or advanced level? Sometimes this is indicated by such words as "Junior" or "Senior" in the class title. Other jurisdictions use Roman numerals to designate the level – Clerk I, Clerk II, for example. The word "Supervisor" sometimes appears in the title. If the level is not indicated by the title, check the description of duties. Will you be working under very close supervision, or will you have responsibility for independent decisions in this work?

4) Choose appropriate study materials

Now that you know the subjects to be examined and the relative amount of each subject to be covered, you can choose suitable study materials. For beginning level jobs, or even advanced ones, if you have a pronounced weakness in some aspect of your training, read a modern, standard textbook in that field. Be sure it is up to date and has general coverage. Such books are normally available at your library, and the librarian will be glad to help you locate one. For entry-level positions, questions of appropriate difficulty are chosen – neither highly advanced questions, nor those too simple. Such questions require careful thought but not advanced training.

If the position for which you are applying is technical or advanced, you will read more advanced, specialized material. If you are already familiar with the basic principles of your field, elementary textbooks would waste your time. Concentrate on advanced textbooks and technical periodicals. Think through the concepts and review difficult problems in your field.

These are all general sources. You can get more ideas on your own initiative, following these leads. For example, training manuals and publications of the government agency which employs workers in your field can be useful, particularly for technical and professional positions. A letter or visit to the government department involved may result in more specific study suggestions, and certainly will provide you with a more definite idea of the exact nature of the position you are seeking.

III. KINDS OF TESTS

Tests are used for purposes other than measuring knowledge and ability to perform specified duties. For some positions, it is equally important to test ability to make adjustments to new situations or to profit from training. In others, basic mental abilities not dependent on information are essential. Questions which test these things may not appear as pertinent to the duties of the position as those which test for knowledge and information. Yet they are often highly important parts of a fair examination. For very general questions, it is almost impossible to help you direct your study efforts. What we can do is to point out some of the more common of these general abilities needed in public service positions and describe some typical questions.

1) General information

Broad, general information has been found useful for predicting job success in some kinds of work. This is tested in a variety of ways, from vocabulary lists to questions about current events. Basic background in some field of work, such as sociology or economics, may be sampled in a group of questions. Often these are principles which have become familiar to most persons through exposure rather than through formal training. It is difficult to advise you how to study for these questions; being alert to the world around you is our best suggestion.

2) Verbal ability

An example of an ability needed in many positions is verbal or language ability. Verbal ability is, in brief, the ability to use and understand words. Vocabulary and grammar tests are typical measures of this ability. Reading comprehension or paragraph interpretation questions are common in many kinds of civil service tests. You are given a paragraph of written material and asked to find its central meaning.

3) Numerical ability
Number skills can be tested by the familiar arithmetic problem, by checking paired lists of numbers to see which are alike and which are different, or by interpreting charts and graphs. In the latter test, a graph may be printed in the test booklet which you are asked to use as the basis for answering questions.

4) Observation
A popular test for law-enforcement positions is the observation test. A picture is shown to you for several minutes, then taken away. Questions about the picture test your ability to observe both details and larger elements.

5) Following directions
In many positions in the public service, the employee must be able to carry out written instructions dependably and accurately. You may be given a chart with several columns, each column listing a variety of information. The questions require you to carry out directions involving the information given in the chart.

6) Skills and aptitudes
Performance tests effectively measure some manual skills and aptitudes. When the skill is one in which you are trained, such as typing or shorthand, you can practice. These tests are often very much like those given in business school or high school courses. For many of the other skills and aptitudes, however, no short-time preparation can be made. Skills and abilities natural to you or that you have developed throughout your lifetime are being tested.

Many of the general questions just described provide all the data needed to answer the questions and ask you to use your reasoning ability to find the answers. Your best preparation for these tests, as well as for tests of facts and ideas, is to be at your physical and mental best. You, no doubt, have your own methods of getting into an exam-taking mood and keeping "in shape." The next section lists some ideas on this subject.

IV. KINDS OF QUESTIONS

Only rarely is the "essay" question, which you answer in narrative form, used in civil service tests. Civil service tests are usually of the short-answer type. Full instructions for answering these questions will be given to you at the examination. But in case this is your first experience with short-answer questions and separate answer sheets, here is what you need to know:

1) Multiple-choice Questions
Most popular of the short-answer questions is the "multiple choice" or "best answer" question. It can be used, for example, to test for factual knowledge, ability to solve problems or judgment in meeting situations found at work.
A multiple-choice question is normally one of three types—
- It can begin with an incomplete statement followed by several possible endings. You are to find the one ending which *best* completes the statement, although some of the others may not be entirely wrong.
- It can also be a complete statement in the form of a question which is answered by choosing one of the statements listed.

- It can be in the form of a problem – again you select the best answer.

Here is an example of a multiple-choice question with a discussion which should give you some clues as to the method for choosing the right answer:

When an employee has a complaint about his assignment, the action which will *best* help him overcome his difficulty is to
    A. discuss his difficulty with his coworkers
    B. take the problem to the head of the organization
    C. take the problem to the person who gave him the assignment
    D. say nothing to anyone about his complaint

In answering this question, you should study each of the choices to find which is best. Consider choice "A" – Certainly an employee may discuss his complaint with fellow employees, but no change or improvement can result, and the complaint remains unresolved. Choice "B" is a poor choice since the head of the organization probably does not know what assignment you have been given, and taking your problem to him is known as "going over the head" of the supervisor. The supervisor, or person who made the assignment, is the person who can clarify it or correct any injustice. Choice "C" is, therefore, correct. To say nothing, as in choice "D," is unwise. Supervisors have and interest in knowing the problems employees are facing, and the employee is seeking a solution to his problem.

2) True/False Questions

The "true/false" or "right/wrong" form of question is sometimes used. Here a complete statement is given. Your job is to decide whether the statement is right or wrong.

SAMPLE: A roaming cell-phone call to a nearby city costs less than a non-roaming call to a distant city.

This statement is wrong, or false, since roaming calls are more expensive.
This is not a complete list of all possible question forms, although most of the others are variations of these common types. You will always get complete directions for answering questions. Be sure you understand *how* to mark your answers – ask questions until you do.

V. RECORDING YOUR ANSWERS

Computer terminals are used more and more today for many different kinds of exams.
For an examination with very few applicants, you may be told to record your answers in the test booklet itself. Separate answer sheets are much more common. If this separate answer sheet is to be scored by machine – and this is often the case – it is highly important that you mark your answers correctly in order to get credit.
An electronic scoring machine is often used in civil service offices because of the speed with which papers can be scored. Machine-scored answer sheets must be marked with a pencil, which will be given to you. This pencil has a high graphite content which responds to the electronic scoring machine. As a matter of fact, stray dots may register as answers, so do not let your pencil rest on the answer sheet while you are pondering the correct answer. Also, if your pencil lead breaks or is otherwise defective, ask for another.

Since the answer sheet will be dropped in a slot in the scoring machine, be careful not to bend the corners or get the paper crumpled.

The answer sheet normally has five vertical columns of numbers, with 30 numbers to a column. These numbers correspond to the question numbers in your test booklet. After each number, going across the page are four or five pairs of dotted lines. These short dotted lines have small letters or numbers above them. The first two pairs may also have a "T" or "F" above the letters. This indicates that the first two pairs only are to be used if the questions are of the true-false type. If the questions are multiple choice, disregard the "T" and "F" and pay attention only to the small letters or numbers.

Answer your questions in the manner of the sample that follows:

32. The largest city in the United States is
    A. Washington, D.C.
    B. New York City
    C. Chicago
    D. Detroit
    E. San Francisco

1) Choose the answer you think is best. (New York City is the largest, so "B" is correct.)
2) Find the row of dotted lines numbered the same as the question you are answering. (Find row number 32)
3) Find the pair of dotted lines corresponding to the answer. (Find the pair of lines under the mark "B.")
4) Make a solid black mark between the dotted lines.

VI. BEFORE THE TEST

Common sense will help you find procedures to follow to get ready for an examination. Too many of us, however, overlook these sensible measures. Indeed, nervousness and fatigue have been found to be the most serious reasons why applicants fail to do their best on civil service tests. Here is a list of reminders:

- Begin your preparation early – Don't wait until the last minute to go scurrying around for books and materials or to find out what the position is all about.
- Prepare continuously – An hour a night for a week is better than an all-night cram session. This has been definitely established. What is more, a night a week for a month will return better dividends than crowding your study into a shorter period of time.
- Locate the place of the exam – You have been sent a notice telling you when and where to report for the examination. If the location is in a different town or otherwise unfamiliar to you, it would be well to inquire the best route and learn something about the building.
- Relax the night before the test – Allow your mind to rest. Do not study at all that night. Plan some mild recreation or diversion; then go to bed early and get a good night's sleep.
- Get up early enough to make a leisurely trip to the place for the test – This way unforeseen events, traffic snarls, unfamiliar buildings, etc. will not upset you.
- Dress comfortably – A written test is not a fashion show. You will be known by number and not by name, so wear something comfortable.

- Leave excess paraphernalia at home – Shopping bags and odd bundles will get in your way. You need bring only the items mentioned in the official notice you received; usually everything you need is provided. Do not bring reference books to the exam. They will only confuse those last minutes and be taken away from you when in the test room.
- Arrive somewhat ahead of time – If because of transportation schedules you must get there very early, bring a newspaper or magazine to take your mind off yourself while waiting.
- Locate the examination room – When you have found the proper room, you will be directed to the seat or part of the room where you will sit. Sometimes you are given a sheet of instructions to read while you are waiting. Do not fill out any forms until you are told to do so; just read them and be prepared.
- Relax and prepare to listen to the instructions
- If you have any physical problem that may keep you from doing your best, be sure to tell the test administrator. If you are sick or in poor health, you really cannot do your best on the exam. You can come back and take the test some other time.

VII. AT THE TEST

The day of the test is here and you have the test booklet in your hand. The temptation to get going is very strong. Caution! There is more to success than knowing the right answers. You must know how to identify your papers and understand variations in the type of short-answer question used in this particular examination. Follow these suggestions for maximum results from your efforts:

1) Cooperate with the monitor

The test administrator has a duty to create a situation in which you can be as much at ease as possible. He will give instructions, tell you when to begin, check to see that you are marking your answer sheet correctly, and so on. He is not there to guard you, although he will see that your competitors do not take unfair advantage. He wants to help you do your best.

2) Listen to all instructions

Don't jump the gun! Wait until you understand all directions. In most civil service tests you get more time than you need to answer the questions. So don't be in a hurry. Read each word of instructions until you clearly understand the meaning. Study the examples, listen to all announcements and follow directions. Ask questions if you do not understand what to do.

3) Identify your papers

Civil service exams are usually identified by number only. You will be assigned a number; you must not put your name on your test papers. Be sure to copy your number correctly. Since more than one exam may be given, copy your exact examination title.

4) Plan your time

Unless you are told that a test is a "speed" or "rate of work" test, speed itself is usually not important. Time enough to answer all the questions will be provided, but this does not mean that you have all day. An overall time limit has been set. Divide the total time (in minutes) by the number of questions to determine the approximate time you have for each question.

5) Do not linger over difficult questions

If you come across a difficult question, mark it with a paper clip (useful to have along) and come back to it when you have been through the booklet. One caution if you do this – be sure to skip a number on your answer sheet as well. Check often to be sure that you have not lost your place and that you are marking in the row numbered the same as the question you are answering.

6) Read the questions

Be sure you know what the question asks! Many capable people are unsuccessful because they failed to *read* the questions correctly.

7) Answer all questions

Unless you have been instructed that a penalty will be deducted for incorrect answers, it is better to guess than to omit a question.

8) Speed tests

It is often better NOT to guess on speed tests. It has been found that on timed tests people are tempted to spend the last few seconds before time is called in marking answers at random – without even reading them – in the hope of picking up a few extra points. To discourage this practice, the instructions may warn you that your score will be "corrected" for guessing. That is, a penalty will be applied. The incorrect answers will be deducted from the correct ones, or some other penalty formula will be used.

9) Review your answers

If you finish before time is called, go back to the questions you guessed or omitted to give them further thought. Review other answers if you have time.

10) Return your test materials

If you are ready to leave before others have finished or time is called, take ALL your materials to the monitor and leave quietly. Never take any test material with you. The monitor can discover whose papers are not complete, and taking a test booklet may be grounds for disqualification.

VIII. EXAMINATION TECHNIQUES

1) Read the general instructions carefully. These are usually printed on the first page of the exam booklet. As a rule, these instructions refer to the timing of the examination; the fact that you should not start work until the signal and must stop work at a signal, etc. If there are any *special* instructions, such as a choice of questions to be answered, make sure that you note this instruction carefully.

2) When you are ready to start work on the examination, that is as soon as the signal has been given, read the instructions to each question booklet, underline any key words or phrases, such as *least, best, outline, describe* and the like. In this way you will tend to answer as requested rather than discover on reviewing your paper that you *listed without describing*, that you selected the *worst* choice rather than the *best* choice, etc.

3) If the examination is of the objective or multiple-choice type – that is, each question will also give a series of possible answers: A, B, C or D, and you are called upon to select the best answer and write the letter next to that answer on your answer paper – it is advisable to start answering each question in turn. There may be anywhere from 50 to 100 such questions in the three or four hours allotted and you can see how much time would be taken if you read through all the questions before beginning to answer any. Furthermore, if you come across a question or group of questions which you know would be difficult to answer, it would undoubtedly affect your handling of all the other questions.

4) If the examination is of the essay type and contains but a few questions, it is a moot point as to whether you should read all the questions before starting to answer any one. Of course, if you are given a choice – say five out of seven and the like – then it is essential to read all the questions so you can eliminate the two that are most difficult. If, however, you are asked to answer all the questions, there may be danger in trying to answer the easiest one first because you may find that you will spend too much time on it. The best technique is to answer the first question, then proceed to the second, etc.

5) Time your answers. Before the exam begins, write down the time it started, then add the time allowed for the examination and write down the time it must be completed, then divide the time available somewhat as follows:
    - If 3-1/2 hours are allowed, that would be 210 minutes. If you have 80 objective-type questions, that would be an average of 2-1/2 minutes per question. Allow yourself no more than 2 minutes per question, or a total of 160 minutes, which will permit about 50 minutes to review.
    - If for the time allotment of 210 minutes there are 7 essay questions to answer, that would average about 30 minutes a question. Give yourself only 25 minutes per question so that you have about 35 minutes to review.

6) The most important instruction is to *read each question* and make sure you know what is wanted. The second most important instruction is to *time yourself properly* so that you answer every question. The third most important instruction is to *answer every question*. Guess if you have to but include something for each question. Remember that you will receive no credit for a blank and will probably receive some credit if you write something in answer to an essay question. If you guess a letter – say "B" for a multiple-choice question – you may have guessed right. If you leave a blank as an answer to a multiple-choice question, the examiners may respect your feelings but it will not add a point to your score. Some exams may penalize you for wrong answers, so in such cases *only*, you may not want to guess unless you have some basis for your answer.

7) Suggestions
    a. Objective-type questions
        1. Examine the question booklet for proper sequence of pages and questions
        2. Read all instructions carefully
        3. Skip any question which seems too difficult; return to it after all other questions have been answered
        4. Apportion your time properly; do not spend too much time on any single question or group of questions

5. Note and underline key words – *all, most, fewest, least, best, worst, same, opposite,* etc.
6. Pay particular attention to negatives
7. Note unusual option, e.g., unduly long, short, complex, different or similar in content to the body of the question
8. Observe the use of "hedging" words – *probably, may, most likely,* etc.
9. Make sure that your answer is put next to the same number as the question
10. Do not second-guess unless you have good reason to believe the second answer is definitely more correct
11. Cross out original answer if you decide another answer is more accurate; do not erase until you are ready to hand your paper in
12. Answer all questions; guess unless instructed otherwise
13. Leave time for review

  b. Essay questions
    1. Read each question carefully
    2. Determine exactly what is wanted. Underline key words or phrases.
    3. Decide on outline or paragraph answer
    4. Include many different points and elements unless asked to develop any one or two points or elements
    5. Show impartiality by giving pros and cons unless directed to select one side only
    6. Make and write down any assumptions you find necessary to answer the questions
    7. Watch your English, grammar, punctuation and choice of words
    8. Time your answers; don't crowd material

8) Answering the essay question

Most essay questions can be answered by framing the specific response around several key words or ideas. Here are a few such key words or ideas:

M's: manpower, materials, methods, money, management
P's: purpose, program, policy, plan, procedure, practice, problems, pitfalls, personnel, public relations

  a. Six basic steps in handling problems:
    1. Preliminary plan and background development
    2. Collect information, data and facts
    3. Analyze and interpret information, data and facts
    4. Analyze and develop solutions as well as make recommendations
    5. Prepare report and sell recommendations
    6. Install recommendations and follow up effectiveness

  b. Pitfalls to avoid
    1. *Taking things for granted* – A statement of the situation does not necessarily imply that each of the elements is necessarily true; for example, a complaint may be invalid and biased so that all that can be taken for granted is that a complaint has been registered

2. *Considering only one side of a situation* – Wherever possible, indicate several alternatives and then point out the reasons you selected the best one
3. *Failing to indicate follow up* – Whenever your answer indicates action on your part, make certain that you will take proper follow-up action to see how successful your recommendations, procedures or actions turn out to be
4. *Taking too long in answering any single question* – Remember to time your answers properly

IX. AFTER THE TEST

Scoring procedures differ in detail among civil service jurisdictions although the general principles are the same. Whether the papers are hand-scored or graded by machine we have described, they are nearly always graded by number. That is, the person who marks the paper knows only the number – never the name – of the applicant. Not until all the papers have been graded will they be matched with names. If other tests, such as training and experience or oral interview ratings have been given, scores will be combined. Different parts of the examination usually have different weights. For example, the written test might count 60 percent of the final grade, and a rating of training and experience 40 percent. In many jurisdictions, veterans will have a certain number of points added to their grades.

After the final grade has been determined, the names are placed in grade order and an eligible list is established. There are various methods for resolving ties between those who get the same final grade – probably the most common is to place first the name of the person whose application was received first. Job offers are made from the eligible list in the order the names appear on it. You will be notified of your grade and your rank as soon as all these computations have been made. This will be done as rapidly as possible.

People who are found to meet the requirements in the announcement are called "eligibles." Their names are put on a list of eligible candidates. An eligible's chances of getting a job depend on how high he stands on this list and how fast agencies are filling jobs from the list.

When a job is to be filled from a list of eligibles, the agency asks for the names of people on the list of eligibles for that job. When the civil service commission receives this request, it sends to the agency the names of the three people highest on this list. Or, if the job to be filled has specialized requirements, the office sends the agency the names of the top three persons who meet these requirements from the general list.

The appointing officer makes a choice from among the three people whose names were sent to him. If the selected person accepts the appointment, the names of the others are put back on the list to be considered for future openings.

That is the rule in hiring from all kinds of eligible lists, whether they are for typist, carpenter, chemist, or something else. For every vacancy, the appointing officer has his choice of any one of the top three eligibles on the list. This explains why the person whose name is on top of the list sometimes does not get an appointment when some of the persons lower on the list do. If the appointing officer chooses the second or third eligible, the No. 1 eligible does not get a job at once, but stays on the list until he is appointed or the list is terminated.

X. HOW TO PASS THE INTERVIEW TEST

The examination for which you applied requires an oral interview test. You have already taken the written test and you are now being called for the interview test – the final part of the formal examination.

You may think that it is not possible to prepare for an interview test and that there are no procedures to follow during an interview. Our purpose is to point out some things you can do in advance that will help you and some good rules to follow and pitfalls to avoid while you are being interviewed.

What is an interview supposed to test?

The written examination is designed to test the technical knowledge and competence of the candidate; the oral is designed to evaluate intangible qualities, not readily measured otherwise, and to establish a list showing the relative fitness of each candidate – as measured against his competitors – for the position sought. Scoring is not on the basis of "right" and "wrong," but on a sliding scale of values ranging from "not passable" to "outstanding." As a matter of fact, it is possible to achieve a relatively low score without a single "incorrect" answer because of evident weakness in the qualities being measured.

Occasionally, an examination may consist entirely of an oral test – either an individual or a group oral. In such cases, information is sought concerning the technical knowledges and abilities of the candidate, since there has been no written examination for this purpose. More commonly, however, an oral test is used to supplement a written examination.

Who conducts interviews?

The composition of oral boards varies among different jurisdictions. In nearly all, a representative of the personnel department serves as chairman. One of the members of the board may be a representative of the department in which the candidate would work. In some cases, "outside experts" are used, and, frequently, a businessman or some other representative of the general public is asked to serve. Labor and management or other special groups may be represented. The aim is to secure the services of experts in the appropriate field.

However the board is composed, it is a good idea (and not at all improper or unethical) to ascertain in advance of the interview who the members are and what groups they represent. When you are introduced to them, you will have some idea of their backgrounds and interests, and at least you will not stutter and stammer over their names.

What should be done before the interview?

While knowledge about the board members is useful and takes some of the surprise element out of the interview, there is other preparation which is more substantive. It *is* possible to prepare for an oral interview – in several ways:

1) Keep a copy of your application and review it carefully before the interview

This may be the only document before the oral board, and the starting point of the interview. Know what education and experience you have listed there, and the sequence and dates of all of it. Sometimes the board will ask you to review the highlights of your experience for them; you should not have to hem and haw doing it.

2) Study the class specification and the examination announcement

Usually, the oral board has one or both of these to guide them. The qualities, characteristics or knowledges required by the position sought are stated in these documents. They offer valuable clues as to the nature of the oral interview. For example, if the job involves supervisory responsibilities, the announcement will usually indicate that knowledge of modern supervisory methods and the qualifications of the candidate as a supervisor will be tested. If so, you can expect such questions, frequently in the form of a hypothetical situation which you are expected to solve. NEVER go into an oral without knowledge of the duties and responsibilities of the job you seek.

3) Think through each qualification required

Try to visualize the kind of questions you would ask if you were a board member. How well could you answer them? Try especially to appraise your own knowledge and background in each area, *measured against the job sought*, and identify any areas in which you are weak. Be critical and realistic – do not flatter yourself.

4) Do some general reading in areas in which you feel you may be weak

For example, if the job involves supervision and your past experience has NOT, some general reading in supervisory methods and practices, particularly in the field of human relations, might be useful. Do NOT study agency procedures or detailed manuals. The oral board will be testing your understanding and capacity, not your memory.

5) Get a good night's sleep and watch your general health and mental attitude

You will want a clear head at the interview. Take care of a cold or any other minor ailment, and of course, no hangovers.

What should be done on the day of the interview?

Now comes the day of the interview itself. Give yourself plenty of time to get there. Plan to arrive somewhat ahead of the scheduled time, particularly if your appointment is in the fore part of the day. If a previous candidate fails to appear, the board might be ready for you a bit early. By early afternoon an oral board is almost invariably behind schedule if there are many candidates, and you may have to wait. Take along a book or magazine to read, or your application to review, but leave any extraneous material in the waiting room when you go in for your interview. In any event, relax and compose yourself.

The matter of dress is important. The board is forming impressions about you – from your experience, your manners, your attitude, and your appearance. Give your personal appearance careful attention. Dress your best, but not your flashiest. Choose conservative, appropriate clothing, and be sure it is immaculate. This is a business interview, and your appearance should indicate that you regard it as such. Besides, being well groomed and properly dressed will help boost your confidence.

Sooner or later, someone will call your name and escort you into the interview room. *This is it.* From here on you are on your own. It is too late for any more preparation. But remember, you asked for this opportunity to prove your fitness, and you are here because your request was granted.

What happens when you go in?

The usual sequence of events will be as follows: The clerk (who is often the board stenographer) will introduce you to the chairman of the oral board, who will introduce you to the other members of the board. Acknowledge the introductions before you sit down. Do not be surprised if you find a microphone facing you or a stenotypist sitting by. Oral interviews are usually recorded in the event of an appeal or other review.

Usually the chairman of the board will open the interview by reviewing the highlights of your education and work experience from your application – primarily for the benefit of the other members of the board, as well as to get the material into the record. Do not interrupt or comment unless there is an error or significant misinterpretation; if that is the case, do not hesitate. But do not quibble about insignificant matters. Also, he will usually ask you some question about your education, experience or your present job – partly to get you to start talking and to establish the interviewing "rapport." He may start the actual questioning, or turn it over to one of the other members. Frequently, each member undertakes the questioning on a particular area, one in which he is perhaps most competent, so you can expect each member to participate in the examination. Because time is limited, you may also expect some rather abrupt switches in the direction the questioning takes, so do not be upset by it. Normally, a board member will not pursue a single line of questioning unless he discovers a particular strength or weakness.

After each member has participated, the chairman will usually ask whether any member has any further questions, then will ask you if you have anything you wish to add. Unless you are expecting this question, it may floor you. Worse, it may start you off on an extended, extemporaneous speech. The board is not usually seeking more information. The question is principally to offer you a last opportunity to present further qualifications or to indicate that you have nothing to add. So, if you feel that a significant qualification or characteristic has been overlooked, it is proper to point it out in a sentence or so. Do not compliment the board on the thoroughness of their examination – they have been sketchy, and you know it. If you wish, merely say, "No thank you, I have nothing further to add." This is a point where you can "talk yourself out" of a good impression or fail to present an important bit of information. Remember, *you close the interview yourself.*

The chairman will then say, "That is all, Mr. _____, thank you." Do not be startled; the interview is over, and quicker than you think. Thank him, gather your belongings and take your leave. Save your sigh of relief for the other side of the door.

How to put your best foot forward

Throughout this entire process, you may feel that the board individually and collectively is trying to pierce your defenses, seek out your hidden weaknesses and embarrass and confuse you. Actually, this is not true. They are obliged to make an appraisal of your qualifications for the job you are seeking, and they want to see you in your best light. Remember, they must interview all candidates and a non-cooperative candidate may become a failure in spite of their best efforts to bring out his qualifications. Here are 15 suggestions that will help you:

1) Be natural – Keep your attitude confident, not cocky

If you are not confident that you can do the job, do not expect the board to be. Do not apologize for your weaknesses, try to bring out your strong points. The board is interested in a positive, not negative, presentation. Cockiness will antagonize any board member and make him wonder if you are covering up a weakness by a false show of strength.

2) Get comfortable, but don't lounge or sprawl

Sit erectly but not stiffly. A careless posture may lead the board to conclude that you are careless in other things, or at least that you are not impressed by the importance of the occasion. Either conclusion is natural, even if incorrect. Do not fuss with your clothing, a pencil or an ashtray. Your hands may occasionally be useful to emphasize a point; do not let them become a point of distraction.

3) Do not wisecrack or make small talk

This is a serious situation, and your attitude should show that you consider it as such. Further, the time of the board is limited – they do not want to waste it, and neither should you.

4) Do not exaggerate your experience or abilities

In the first place, from information in the application or other interviews and sources, the board may know more about you than you think. Secondly, you probably will not get away with it. An experienced board is rather adept at spotting such a situation, so do not take the chance.

5) If you know a board member, do not make a point of it, yet do not hide it

Certainly you are not fooling him, and probably not the other members of the board. Do not try to take advantage of your acquaintanceship – it will probably do you little good.

6) Do not dominate the interview

Let the board do that. They will give you the clues – do not assume that you have to do all the talking. Realize that the board has a number of questions to ask you, and do not try to take up all the interview time by showing off your extensive knowledge of the answer to the first one.

7) Be attentive

You only have 20 minutes or so, and you should keep your attention at its sharpest throughout. When a member is addressing a problem or question to you, give him your undivided attention. Address your reply principally to him, but do not exclude the other board members.

8) Do not interrupt

A board member may be stating a problem for you to analyze. He will ask you a question when the time comes. Let him state the problem, and wait for the question.

9) Make sure you understand the question

Do not try to answer until you are sure what the question is. If it is not clear, restate it in your own words or ask the board member to clarify it for you. However, do not haggle about minor elements.

10) Reply promptly but not hastily

A common entry on oral board rating sheets is "candidate responded readily," or "candidate hesitated in replies." Respond as promptly and quickly as you can, but do not jump to a hasty, ill-considered answer.

11) Do not be peremptory in your answers

A brief answer is proper – but do not fire your answer back. That is a losing game from your point of view. The board member can probably ask questions much faster than you can answer them.

12) Do not try to create the answer you think the board member wants

He is interested in what kind of mind you have and how it works – not in playing games. Furthermore, he can usually spot this practice and will actually grade you down on it.

13) Do not switch sides in your reply merely to agree with a board member

Frequently, a member will take a contrary position merely to draw you out and to see if you are willing and able to defend your point of view. Do not start a debate, yet do not surrender a good position. If a position is worth taking, it is worth defending.

14) Do not be afraid to admit an error in judgment if you are shown to be wrong

The board knows that you are forced to reply without any opportunity for careful consideration. Your answer may be demonstrably wrong. If so, admit it and get on with the interview.

15) Do not dwell at length on your present job

The opening question may relate to your present assignment. Answer the question but do not go into an extended discussion. You are being examined for a *new* job, not your present one. As a matter of fact, try to phrase ALL your answers in terms of the job for which you are being examined.

Basis of Rating

Probably you will forget most of these "do's" and "don'ts" when you walk into the oral interview room. Even remembering them all will not ensure you a passing grade. Perhaps you did not have the qualifications in the first place. But remembering them will help you to put your best foot forward, without treading on the toes of the board members.

Rumor and popular opinion to the contrary notwithstanding, an oral board wants you to make the best appearance possible. They know you are under pressure – but they also want to see how you respond to it as a guide to what your reaction would be under the pressures of the job you seek. They will be influenced by the degree of poise you display, the personal traits you show and the manner in which you respond.

ABOUT THIS BOOK

This book contains tests divided into Examination Sections. Go through each test, answering every question in the margin. We have also attached a sample answer sheet at the back of the book that can be removed and used. At the end of each test look at the answer key and check your answers. On the ones you got wrong, look at the right answer choice and learn. Do not fill in the answers first. Do not memorize the questions and answers, but understand the answer and principles involved. On your test, the questions will likely be different from the samples. Questions are changed and new ones added. If you understand these past questions you should have success with any changes that arise. Tests may consist of several types of questions. We have additional books on each subject should more study be advisable or necessary for you. Finally, the more you study, the better prepared you will be. This book is intended to be the last thing you study before you walk into the examination room. Prior study of relevant texts is also recommended. NLC publishes some of these in our Fundamental Series. Knowledge and good sense are important factors in passing your exam. Good luck also helps. So now study this Passbook, absorb the material contained within and take that knowledge into the examination. Then do your best to pass that exam.

EXAMINATION SECTION

EXAMINATION SECTION
TEST 1

DIRECTIONS: Each question or incomplete statement is followed by several suggested answers or completions. Select the one that BEST answers the question or completes the statement. *PRINT THE LETTER OF THE CORRECT ANSWER IN THE SPACE AT THE RIGHT.*

Questions 1-6.

DIRECTIONS: Questions 1 through 6 are to be answered on the basis of the circuit diagram below. All switches are initially open.

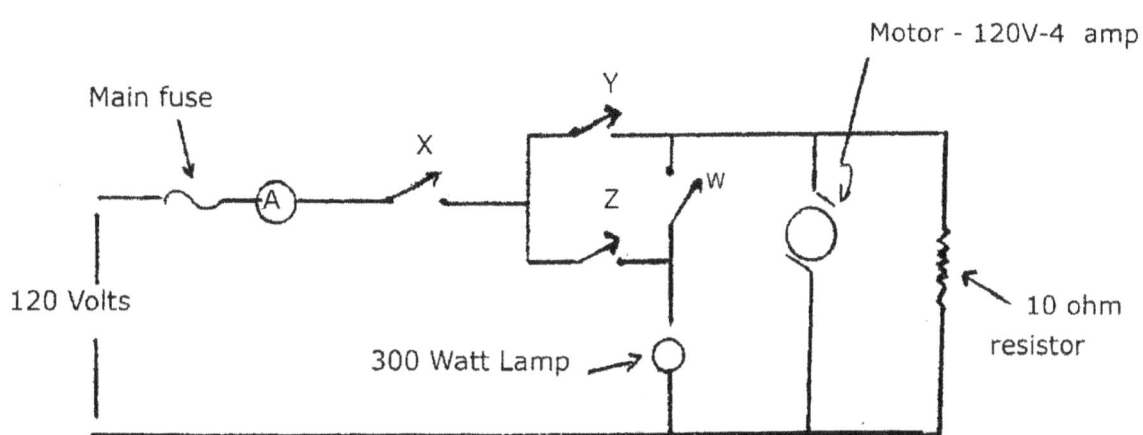

1. To light the 300 watt lamp, the following switches MUST be closed: 1.____

   A. X and Y   B. Y and Z   C. X and Z   D. X and W

2. If all of the switches W, X, Y, and Z are closed, the following will happen: 2.____

   A. The lamp will light and the motor will rotate
   B. The lamp will light and the motor will not rotate
   C. The lamp will not light and the motor will not rotate
   D. A short circuit will occur and the main fuse will blow

3. With 120 volts applied across the 10 ohm resistor, the current drawn by the resistor is _____ amp(s).   3.____

   A. 1/12   B. 1.2   C. 12   D. 1200

4. With 120 volts applied to the 10 ohm resistor, the power used by the resistor is _____ kw.   4.____

   A. 1.44   B. 1.2   C. .144   D. .12

5. The current drawn by the 300 watt lamp when lighted should be APPROXIMATELY _____ amps.   5.____

   A. 2.5   B. 3.6   C. 25   D. 36

6. In the circuit shown, the symbol A is used to indicate a (n)

   A. ammeter
   B. *and* circuit
   C. voltmeter
   D. wattmeter

7. Of the following materials, the BEST conductor of electricity is

   A. iron
   B. copper
   C. aluminum
   D. glass

8. The sum of 6'6", 5'9", and 2' 1 1/2" is

   A. 13'4 1/2"
   B. 13'6 1/2"
   C. 14'4 1/2"
   D. 14'6 1/2"

9.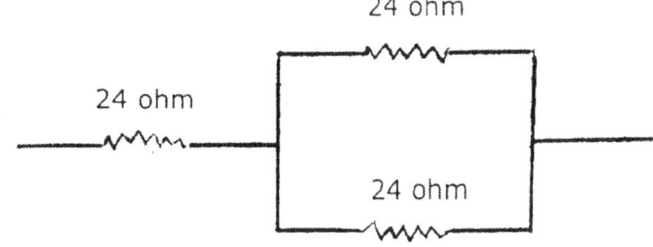

   The equivalent resistance of the three resistors shown in the sketch above is _____ ohms.

   A. 8
   B. 24
   C. 36
   D. 72

10.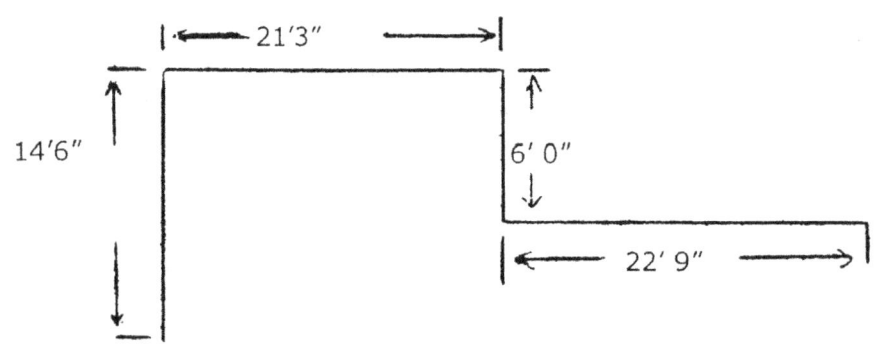

    The TOTAL length of electrical conduit that must be run along the path shown on the diagram above is

    A. 63'8"
    B. 64'6"
    C. 65'6"
    D. 66'8"

11. Of the following electrical devices, the one that is NOT normally used in direct current electrical circuits is a (n)

    A. circuit breaker
    B. double-pole switch
    C. transformer
    D. inverter

12. The number of 120-volt light bulbs that should NORMALLY be connected in series across a 600-volt electric line is

    A. 1
    B. 2
    C. 3
    D. 5

13. Of the following motors, the one that does NOT have any brushes is the _____ motor. 13.____

    A. d.c. shunt
    B. d.c. series
    C. squirrel cage induction
    D. compound

14. Of the following materials, the one that is COMMONLY used as an electric heating element in an electric heater is 14.____

    A. zinc
    B. brass
    C. terne plate
    D. nichrome

Questions 15-25.

DIRECTIONS: Questions 15 through 25 are to be answered on the basis of the instruments listed below. Each instrument is listed with an identifying number in front of it.

    1 - Hygrometer
    2 - Ammeter
    3 - Voltmeter
    4 - Wattmeter
    5 - Megger
    6 - Oscilloscope
    7 - Frequency meter
    8 - Micrometer
    9 - Vernier caliper
    10 - Wire gage
    11 - 6-foot folding rule
    12 - Architect's scale
    13 - Planimeter
    14 - Engineer's scale
    15 - Ohmmeter

15. The instrument that should be used to accurately measure the resistance of a 4,700 ohm resistor is Number 15.____

    A. 3 B. 4 C. 7 D. 15

16. To measure the current in an electrical circuit, the instrument that should be used is Number 16.____

    A. 2 B. 7 C. 8 D. 15

17. To measure the insulation resistance of a rubber-covered electrical cable, the instrument that should be used is Number 17.____

    A. 4 B. 5 C. 8 D. 15

18. An AC motor is hooked up to a power distribution box. 18.____
    In order to check the voltage at the motor terminals, the instrument that should be used is Number

    A. 2 B. 3 C. 4 D. 7

19. To measure the shaft diameter of a motor accurately to one-thousandth of an inch, the instrument that should be used is Number 19.____

    A. 8 B. 10 C. 11 D. 14

20. The instrument that should be used to determine whether 25 Hz. or 60 Hz. is present in an electrical circuit is Number 20.____

    A. 4 B. 5 C. 7 D. 8

21. Of the following, the PROPER instrument to use to determine the diameter of the conductor of a piece of electrical hook-up wire is Number

    A. 10   B. 11   C. 12   D. 14

22. The amount of electrical power being used in a balanced three-phase circuit should be measured with Number

    A. 2   B. 3   C. 4   D. 5

23. The electrical wave form at a given point in an electronic circuit can be observed with Number

    A. 2   B. 3   C. 6   D. 7

24. The PROPER instrument to use for measuring the width of a door is Number

    A. 11   B. 12   C. 13   D. 14

25. A one-inch hole with a tolerance of plus or minus three-thousandths is reamed in a steel block.
    The PROPER instrument to use to accurately check the diameter of the hole is Number

    A. 8   B. 9   C. 11   D. 14

KEY (CORRECT ANSWERS)

1. C		11. C	
2. A		12. D	
3. C		13. C	
4. A		14. D	
5. A		15. D	
6. A		16. A	
7. B		17. B	
8. C		18. B	
9. C		19. A	
10. B		20. C	

21. A
22. C
23. C
24. A
25. B

TEST 2

DIRECTIONS: Each question or incomplete statement is followed by several suggested answers or completions. Select the one that BEST answers the question or completes the statement. *PRINT THE LETTER OF THE CORRECT ANSWER IN THE SPACE AT THE RIGHT.*

1. The number of conductors required to connect a 3-phase delta connected heater bank to an electric power panel board is   1.____

    A. 2   B. 3   C. 4   D. 5

2. Of the following, the wire size that is MOST commonly used for branch lighting circuits in homes is _____ A.W.G.   2.____

    A. #12   B. #8   C. #6   D. #4

3. When installing electrical circuits, the tool that should be used to pull wire through a conduit is a   3.____

    A. mandrel   B. snake
    C. rod   D. pulling iron

4. Of the following AC voltages, the LOWEST voltage that a neon test lamp can detect is _____ volts.   4.____

    A. 6   B. 12   C. 80   D. 120

5. Of the following, the BEST procedure to use when storing tools that are subject to rusting is to   5.____

    A. apply a thin coating of soap onto the tools
    B. apply a light coating of oil to the tools
    C. wrap the tools in clean cheesecloth
    D. place the tools in a covered container

6. If a 3 1/2 inch long nail is required to nail wood framing members together, the nail size to use should be   6.____

    A. 2d   B. 4d   C. 16d   D. 60d

7. Of the four motors listed below, the one that can operate only on alternating current is a(n) _____ motor.   7.____

    A. series   B. shunt
    C. compound   D. induction

8. The sum of 1/3 + 2/5 + 5/6 is   8.____

    A. 1 17/30   B. 1 3/5   C. 1 15/24   D. 1 5/6

9. Of the following instruments, the one that should be used to measure the state of charge of a lead-acid storage battery is a(n)   9.____

    A. ammeter   B. ohmmeter
    C. hydrometer   D. thermometer

10. If three 1 1/2 volt dry cell batteries are wired in series, the TOTAL voltage provided by the three batteries is _____ volts.

    A. 1.5   B. 3   C. 4.5   D. 6.0

11. Taking into account time and one-half payment for time over 40 hours of work, the gross pay of an employee who works 43 hours in a week at a rate of pay of $10.68 per hour is

    A. $427.20   B. $459.24   C. $475.26   D. $491.28

12. The sum of 0.365 + 3.941 + 10.676 + 0.784 is

    A. 13.766   B. 15.666   C. 15.756   D. 15.766

13. In order to transmit mechanical power between two rotating shafts at right angles to each other, two gears are used. Of the following, the type of gears that should be used are _____ gears.

    A. herringbone   B. spur
    C. bevel   D. rack and pinion

14. To properly ground the service electrical equipment in a building, a ground connection should be made to _____ the building.

    A. the waste or soil line leaving
    B. the vent line going to the exterior of
    C. any steel beam in
    D. the cold water line entering

15. The area of the triangle shown at the right is _____ square inches.
    A. 120
    B. 240
    C. 360
    D. 480

Questions 16-25.

DIRECTIONS: Questions 16 through 25 are to be answered on the basis of the tools shown on the next page. The tools are not shown to scale. Each tool is shown with an identifying number alongside it.

3 (#2)

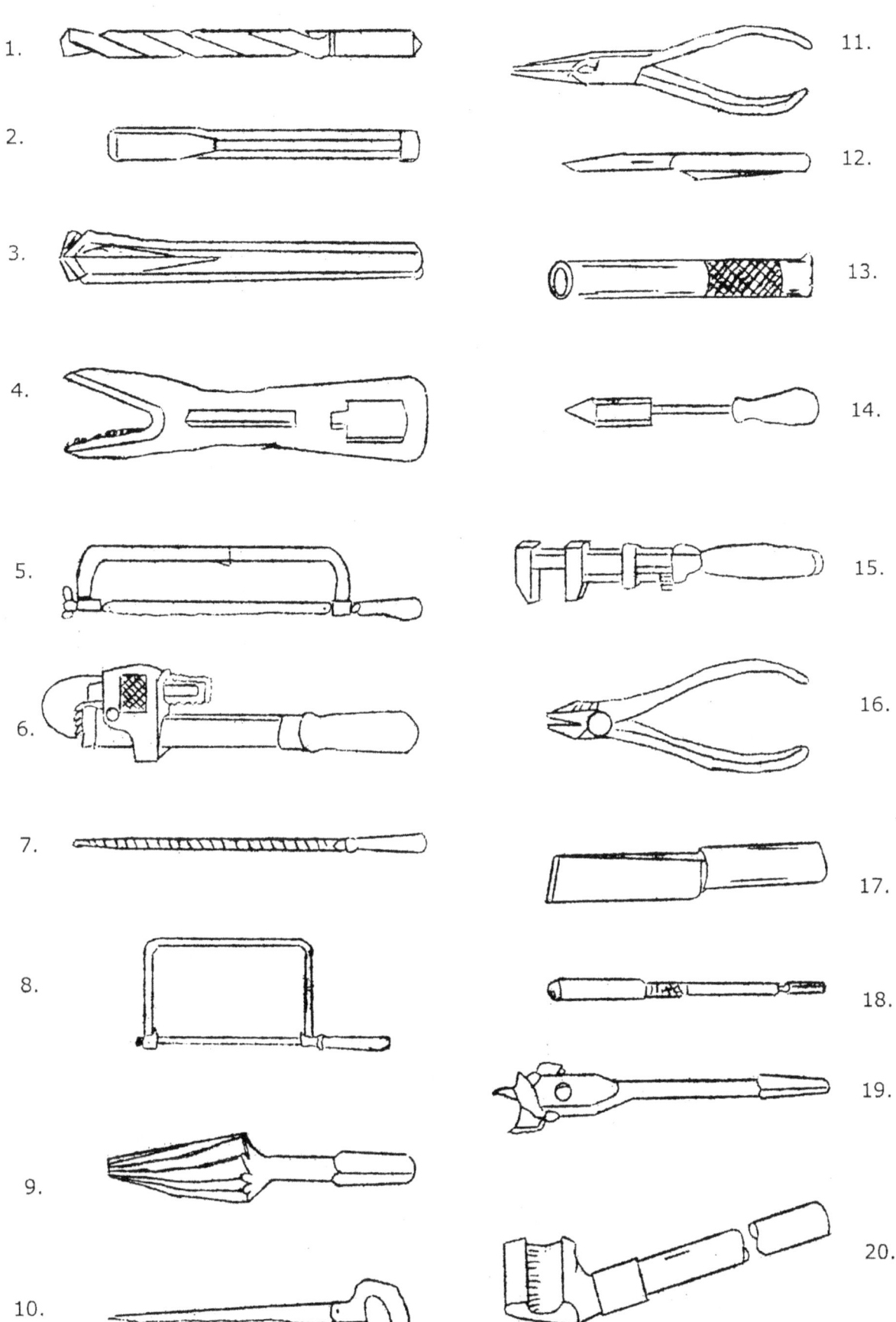

16. The tool that should be used for cutting thin wall steel conduit is Number
    A. 5   B. 8   C. 10   D. 16

17. The tool that should be used for cutting a 1 7/8 inch diameter hole in a wood joist is Number
    A. 3   B. 9   C. 14   D. 19

18. The tool that should be used for soldering splices in electrical wire is Number
    A. 3   B. 7   C. 13   D. 14

19. After cutting off a piece of 3/4 inch diameter electrical conduit, the tool that should be used for removing a burr from the inside of the conduit is Number
    A. 9   B. 11   C. 12   D. 14

20. The tool that should be used for turning a coupling onto a threaded conduit is Number
    A. 6   B. 11   C. 15   D. 16

21. The tool that should be used for cutting wood lathing in plaster walls is Number
    A. 5   B. 7   C. 10   D. 12

22. The tool that should be used for drilling a 3/8 inch diameter hole in a steel beam is Number
    A. 1   B. 2   C. 3   D. 9

23. Of the following, the BEST tool to use for stripping insulation from electrical hook-up wire is Number
    A. 11   B. 12   C. 15   D. 20

24. The tool that should be used for bending an electrical wire around a terminal post is Number
    A. 4   B. 11   C. 15   D. 16

25. The tool that should be used for cutting electrical hookup wire is Number
    A. 5   B. 12   C. 16   D. 17

KEY (CORRECT ANSWERS)

1. B
2. A
3. B
4. C
5. B

6. C
7. D
8. A
9. C
10. C

11. C
12. D
13. C
14. D
15. A

16. A
17. D
18. D
19. A
20. A

21. C
22. A
23. B
24. B
25. C

TEST 3

DIRECTIONS: Each question or incomplete statement is followed by several suggested answers or completions. Select the one that BEST answers the question or completes the statement. *PRINT THE LETTER OF THE CORRECT ANSWER IN THE SPACE AT THE RIGHT.*

1. An electric circuit has current flowing through it. The panel board switch feeding the circuit is opened, causing arcing across the switch contacts.
   Generally, this arcing is caused by

   A. a lack of energy storage in the circuit
   B. electrical energy stored by a capacitor
   C. electrical energy stored by a resistor
   D. magnetic energy induced by an inductance

   1.___

2. MOST filter capacitors in radios have a capacity rating given in

   A. microvolts   B. milliamps
   C. millihenries   D. microfarads

   2.___

3. Of the following, the electrical wire size that is COMMONLY used for telephone circuits is _____ A.W.G.

   A. #6   B. #10   C. #12   D. #22

   3.___

Questions 4-9.

DIRECTIONS: Questions 4 through 9 are to be answered on the basis of the electrical circuit diagram shown below, where letters are used to identify various circuit components.

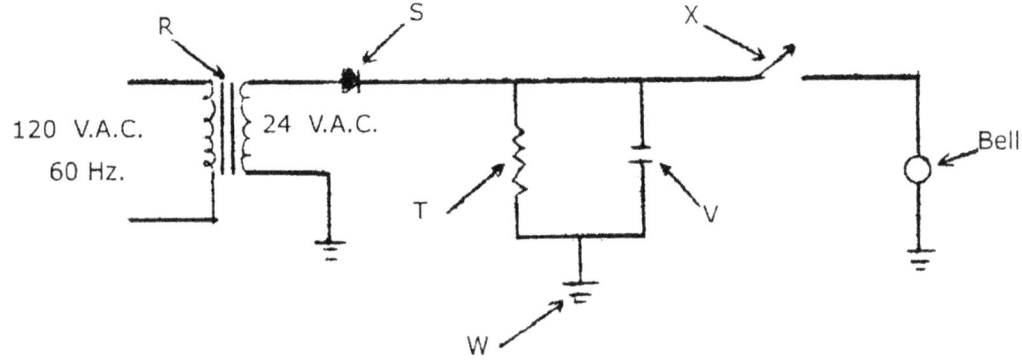

4. The device indicated by the letter R is a

   A. capacitor   B. converter
   C. resistor   D. transformer

   4.___

5. The device indicated by the letter S is a

   A. transistor   B. diode
   C. thermistor   D. directional relay

   5.___

6. The devices indicated by the letters T and V are used together to _____ components of the secondary current.

   A. reduce the AC
   B. reduce the DC
   C. transform the AC
   D. invert the AC

7. The letter W points to a standard electrical symbol for a

   A. wire
   B. ground
   C. terminal
   D. lightning arrestor

8. Closing switch X will apply the following type of voltage to the bell:

   A. 60 Hz. AC
   B. DC
   C. pulsating AC
   D. 120 Hz. AC

9. The circuit shown contains a _____ rectifier.

   A. mercury-arc
   B. full-wave
   C. bridge
   D. half-wave

10. A bolt specified as 1/4-28 means the following:
    The

    A. bolt is 1/4 inch in diameter and has 28 threads per inch
    B. bolt is 1/4 inch in diameter and is 2.8 inches long
    C. bolt is 1/4 inch long and has 28 threads
    D. threaded portion of the bolt is 1/4 inch long and has 28 threads per inch

11. When cutting 0.045-inch thickness sheet metal, it is BEST to use a hacksaw blade that has _____ teeth per inch.

    A. 7   B. 12   C. 18   D. 32

12. To accurately tighten a bolt to 28 foot-pounds, it is BEST to use a(n) _____ wrench.

    A. pipe   B. open end   C. box   D. torque

13. When bending a 2-inch diameter conduit, the CORRECT tool to use is a

    A. hickey
    B. pipe wrench
    C. hydraulic bender
    D. stock and die

14. When soldering two #20 A.W.G. copper wires together to form a splice, the solder that SHOULD be used is _____ solder.

    A. acid-core
    B. solid-core
    C. rosin-core
    D. liquid

15. A bathroom heating unit draws 10 amperes at 115 volts.
    The hot resistance of the heating unit should be _____ ohms.

    A. .08   B. 8   C. 11.5   D. 1150

16. Of the following materials, the one that is NOT suitable as an electrical insulator is

    A. glass   B. mica   C. rubber   D. platinum

17. An air conditioning unit is rated at 1000 watts. The unit is run for 10 hours per day, five days per week.
If the cost for electrical energy is 5 cents per kilowatt-hour, the weekly cost for electricity should be

   A. 25¢ B. 50¢ C. $2.50 D. $25.00

18. If a fuse is protecting the circuit of a 15 ohm electric heater and it is designed to blow out at a current exceeding 10 amperes, the MAXIMUM voltage from among the following that should be applied across the terminals of the heater is _____ volts.

   A. 110 B. 120 C. 160 D. 600

19. Before opening a pneumatic hose connection, it is important to remove pressure from the hose line PRIMARILY to avoid

   A. losing air
   B. personal injury
   C. damage to the hose connection
   D. a build-up of pressure in the air compressor

20. If the scale on a shop drawing is 1/4 inch to the foot, then a part which measures 3 3/8 inches long on the drawing has an ACTUAL length of _____ feet _____ inches.

   A. 12; 6 B. 13; 6 C. 13; 9 D. 14; 9

21. The function that is USUALLY performed by a motor controller is to

   A. start and stop a motor
   B. protect a motor from a short circuit
   C. prevent bearing failure of a motor
   D. control the brush wear in a motor

22. Of the following galvanized sheet metal electrical outlet boxes, the one that is NOT a commonly used size is the _____ box.

   A. 4" square
   B. 4" octagonal
   C. 4" x 2 1/8"
   D. 4" x 1"

23. When soldering a transistor into a circuit, it is MOST important to protect the transistor from

   A. the application of an excess of rosin flux
   B. excessive heat
   C. the application of an excess of solder
   D. too much pressure

24. When installing BX type cable, it is important to protect the wires in the cable from the cut ends of the armored sheath.
The APPROVED method of providing this protection is to

   A. use a fiber or plastic insulating bushing
   B. file the cut ends of the sheath smooth
   C. use a connector where the cable enters a junction box
   D. tie the wires into an Underwriter's knot

25. While lifting a heavy piece of equipment off the floor, a person should NOT

    A. twist his body
    B. grasp it firmly
    C. maintain a solid footing on the ground
    D. bend his knees

26. It is important that metal cabinets and panels that house electrical equipment should be grounded PRIMARILY in order to

    A. prevent short circuits from occurring
    B. keep all circuits at ground potential
    C. minimize shock hazards
    D. reduce the effects of electrolytic corrosion

27. A foreman explains a technical procedure to a new employee. If the employee does not understand the instructions he has received, it would be BEST if he were to

    A. follow the procedure as best he could
    B. ask the foreman to explain it to him again
    C. avoid following the procedure
    D. ask the foreman to give him other work

28. Of the following, the BEST connectors to use when mounting an electrical panel box directly onto a concrete wall are

    A. threaded studs
    B. machine screws
    C. lag screws
    D. expansion bolts

29. Of the following, the BEST instrument to use to measure the small gap between relay contacts is

    A. a micrometer
    B. a feeler gage
    C. inside calipers
    D. a plug gage

30. A POSSIBLE result of mounting a 40 ampere fuse in a fuse box for a circuit requiring a 20 ampere fuse is that the 40 ampere fuse may

    A. provide twice as much protection to the circuit from overloads
    B. blow more easily than the smaller fuse due to an overload
    C. cause serious damage to the circuit from an overload
    D. reduce power consumption in the circuit

KEY (CORRECT ANSWERS)

1.	D	16.	D
2.	D	17.	C
3.	D	18.	B
4.	D	19.	B
5.	B	20.	B
6.	A	21.	A
7.	B	22.	D
8.	B	23.	B
9.	D	24.	A
10.	A	25.	A
11.	D	26.	C
12.	D	27.	B
13.	C	28.	D
14.	C	29.	B
15.	C	30.	C

EXAMINATION SECTION
TEST 1

DIRECTIONS: Each question or incomplete statement is followed by several suggested answers or completions. Select the one that BEST answers the question or completes the statement. *PRINT THE LETTER OF THE CORRECT ANSWER IN THE SPACE AT THE RIGHT.*

1. The combustion efficiency of a boiler can be determined with a CO_2 indicator and the   1._____

    A. under fire draft
    B. boiler room humidity
    C. flue gas temperature
    D. outside air temperature

2. A quick, practical method of determining if the cast-iron waste pipe delivered to a job has been damaged in transit is to   2._____

    A. hydraulically test it
    B. "ring" each length with a hammer
    C. drop each length to see whether it breaks
    D. visually examine the pipe for cracks

3. An electrostatic precipitator is used to   3._____

    A. filter the air supply
    B. remove sludge from the fuel oil
    C. remove particles from the fuel gas
    D. supply samples for an Orsat analysis

4. The PRIMARY cause of cracking and spalling of refractory lining in the furnace of a steam generator is *most likely* due to   4._____

    A. continuous over-firing of boiler
    B. slag accumulation on furnace walls
    C. change in fuel from solid to liquid
    D. uneven heating and cooling within the refractory brick

5. The term "effective temperature" in air conditioning means   5._____

    A. the dry bulb temperature
    B. the average of the wet and dry bulb temperatures
    C. the square root of the product of wet and dry bulb temperatures
    D. an arbitrary index combining the effects of temperature, humidity, and movement

6. The piping in all buildings having dual water distribution systems should be identified by a color coding of _____ for potable water lines and _____ for non-potable water lines.   6._____

    A. green; red
    B. green; yellow
    C. yellow; green
    D. yellow; red

7. The breaking of a component of a machine subjected to excessive vibration is called   7._____

    A. tensile failure
    B. fatigue failure
    C. caustic embrittlement
    D. amplitude failure

2 (#1)

8. The TWO MOST important factors to be considered in selecting fans for ventilating systems are

   A. noise and efficiency
   B. space available and weight
   C. first cost and dimensional bulk
   D. construction and arrangement of drive

9. In the modern power plant deaerator, air is removed from water to

   A. reduce heat losses in the heaters
   B. reduce corrosion of boiler steel due to the air
   C. reduce the load of the main condenser air pumps
   D. prevent pumps from becoming vapor bound

10. The abbreviations BOD, COD, and DO are associated with

    A. flue gas analysis
    B. air pollution control
    C. boiler water treatment
    D. water pollution control

11. The piping of a newly installed drainage system should be tested upon completion of the rough plumbing with a head of water of NOT LESS THAN _____ feet.

    A. 10   B. 15   C. 20   D. 25

12. Of the following statements concerning aquastats, the one which is CORRECT is:

    A. Aquastats may be obtained with either a narrow or wide range of settings
    B. Aquastats have a mercury tube switch which is controlled by the stack switch
    C. An aquastat is a device used to shut down the burner in the event of low water in the boiler
    D. An aquastat should be located about 4 inches above the normal water line of the boiler

13. The SAFEST way to protect the domestic water supply from contamination by sewage or non-potable water is to insert

    A. air gaps
    B. swing connections
    C. double check valves
    D. tanks with overhead discharge

14. The MAIN function of a back-pressure valve which is sometimes found in the connection between a water drain pipe and the sewer system is to

    A. equalize the pressure between the drain pipe and the sewer
    B. prevent sewer water from flowing into the drain pipe
    C. provide pressure to enable waste to reach the sewer
    D. make sure that there is not too much water pressure in the sewer line

15. Boiler water is neutral if its pH value is

    A. 0   B. 1   C. 7   D. 14

16. A domestic hot water mixing or tempering valve should be preceded in the hot water line by a

    A. strainer
    B. foot valve
    C. check valve
    D. steam trap

17. Between a steam boiler and its safety valve there should be

    A. no valve of any type
    B. a gate valve of the same size as the safety valve
    C. a swing check valve of at least the same size as the safety valve
    D. a cock having a clear opening equal in area to the pipe connecting the boiler and safety valve

18. A diagram of horizontal plumbing drainage lines should have cleanouts shown

    A. at least every 25 feet
    B. at least every 100 feet
    C. wherever a basin is located
    D. wherever a change in direction occurs

19. When a Bourdon gauge is used to measure steam pressures, some form of siphon or water seal must be maintained.
    The reason for this is to

    A. obtain "absolute" pressure readings
    B. prevent steam from entering the gage
    C. prevent condensate from entering the gage
    D. obtain readings below atmospheric pressure

20. In a closed heat exchanger, oil is cooled by condensate which is to be returned to a boiler. In order to avoid the possibility of contaminating the condensate with oil should a tube fail in the oil cooler, it would be good practice to

    A. cool the oil by air instead of water
    B. treat the condensate with an oil solvent
    C. keep the oil pressure in the exchanger higher than the water pressure
    D. keep the water pressure in the exchanger higher than the oil pressure

21. A radiator thermostatic trap is used on a vacuum return type of heating system to

    A. release the pocketed air only
    B. reduce the amount of condensate
    C. maintain a predetermined radiator water level
    D. prevent the return of live steam to the return line

22. According to the color coding of piping, fire protection piping should be painted

    A. green   B. yellow   C. purple   D. red

23. The MAIN purpose of a standpipe system is to

    A. supply the roof water tank
    B. provide water for firefighting

C. circulate water for the heating system
D. provide adequate pressure for the water supply

24. The name "Saybolt" is associated with the measurement of

    A. viscosity
    B. Btu content
    C. octane rating
    D. temperature

25. Recirculation of conditioned air in an air-conditioned building is done MAINLY to

    A. reduce refrigeration tonnage required
    B. increase room entrophy
    C. increase air specific humidity
    D. reduce room temperature below the dewpoint

26. In a plumbing installation, vent pipes are GENERALLY used to

    A. prevent the loss of water seal from traps by evaporation
    B. prevent the loss of water seal due to several causes other than evaporation
    C. act as an additional path for liquids to flow through during normal use of a plumbing fixture
    D. prevent the backflow of water in a cross-connection between a drinking water line and a sewage line

27. The designation "150 W" cast on the bonnet of a gate valve is an indication of the

    A. water working temperature
    B. water working pressure
    C. area of the opening in square inches
    D. weight of the valve in pounds

28. In the city, the size soil pipe necessary in a sewage drainage system is determined by the

    A. legal occupancy of the building
    B. vertical height of the soil line
    C. number of restrooms connected to the soil line
    D. number of "fixture units" connected to the soil line

29. Fins or other extended surfaces are used on heat exchanger tubes when

    A. the exchanger is a water-to-water exchanger
    B. water is on one side of the tube and condensing steam on the other side
    C. the surface coefficient of heat transfer on both sides of the tube is high
    D. the surface coefficient of heat transfer on one side of the tube is low compared to the coefficient on the other side of the tube

30. A fusible plug may be put in a fire tube boiler as an emergency device to indicate low water level. The fusible plug is installed so that under normal operating conditions,

    A. both sides are exposed to steam
    B. one side is exposed to water and the other side to steam
    C. one side is exposed to steam and the other side to hot gases
    D. one side is exposed to the water and the other side to hot gases

31. Extra strong wrought-iron pipe, as compared to standard wrought-iron pipe of the same nominal size, has   31.____

    A. the same outside diameter but a smaller inside diameter
    B. the same inside diameter but a larger outside diameter
    C. a larger outside diameter and a smaller inside diameter
    D. larger inside and outside diameters

32. Fans may be rated on a dynamic or a static efficiency basis. The dynamic efficiency would *probably* be   32.____

    A. lower in value because of the energy absorbed by the air velocity
    B. the same as the static in the case of centrifugal blowers running at various speeds
    C. the same as the static in the case of axial flow blowers running at various speeds
    D. higher in value than the static

33. The function of the stack relay in an oil burner installation is to   33.____

    A. regulate the draft over the fire
    B. regulate the flow of fuel oil to the burner
    C. stop the motor if the oil has not ignited
    D. stop the motor if the water or steam pressure is too high

34. The type of centrifugal pump which is inherently balanced for hydraulic thrust is the   34.____

    A. double suction impeller type
    B. single suction impeller type
    C. single stage type
    D. multistage type

35. The specifications for a job using sheet lead calls for "4-lb. sheet lead." This means that each sheet should weigh   35.____

    A. 4 lbs.
    B. 4 lbs. per square
    C. 4 lbs. per square foot
    D. 4 lbs. per cubic inch

36. The total cooling load design conditions for a building are divided for convenience into two components.   36.____
    These are:

    A. infiltration and radiation
    B. sensible heat and latent heat
    C. wet and dry bulb temperatures
    D. solar heat gain and moisture transfer

37. The function of a Hartford loop used on some steam boilers is to   37.____

    A. limit boiler steam pressure
    B. limit temperature of the steam
    C. prevent high water levels in the boiler
    D. prevent back flow of water from the boiler into the return main

38. Vibration from a ventilating blower can be prevented from being transmitted to the duct work by

    A. installing straighteners in the duct
    B. throttling the air supply to the blower
    C. bolting the blower tightly to the duct
    D. installing a canvas sleeve at the blower outlet

39. A specification states that access panels to suspended ceiling will be of metal. The MAIN reason for providing access panels is to

    A. improve the insulation of the ceiling
    B. improve the appearance of the ceiling
    C. make it easier to construct the building
    D. make it easier to maintain the building

40. A plumber on a job reports that the steamfitter has installed a 3" steam line in a location at which the plans show the house trap. On inspecting the job, you should

    A. tell the steamfitter to remove the steam line
    B. study the condition to see if the house trap can be relocated
    C. tell the plumber and steamfitter to work it out between themselves and then report to you
    D. tell the plumber to find another location for the trap because the steamfitter has already completed his work

41. In the installation of any heating system, the MOST important consideration is that

    A. all elements be made of a good grade of cast iron
    B. all radiators and connectors be mounted horizontally
    C. the smallest velocity of flow of heating medium be used
    D. there be proper clearance between hot surfaces and surrounding combustible material

42. Which one of the following is the PRIMARY object in drawing up a set of specifications for materials to be purchased?

    A. Control of quality
    B. Outline of intended use
    C. Establishment of standard sizes
    D. Location and method of inspection.

43. The drawing which should be used as a LEGAL reference when checking completed construction work is the _____ drawing.

    A. contract   B. assembly
    C. working or shop   D. preliminary

Questions 44-50.

DIRECTIONS: Questions 44 through 50 refer to the plumbing drawing shown below.

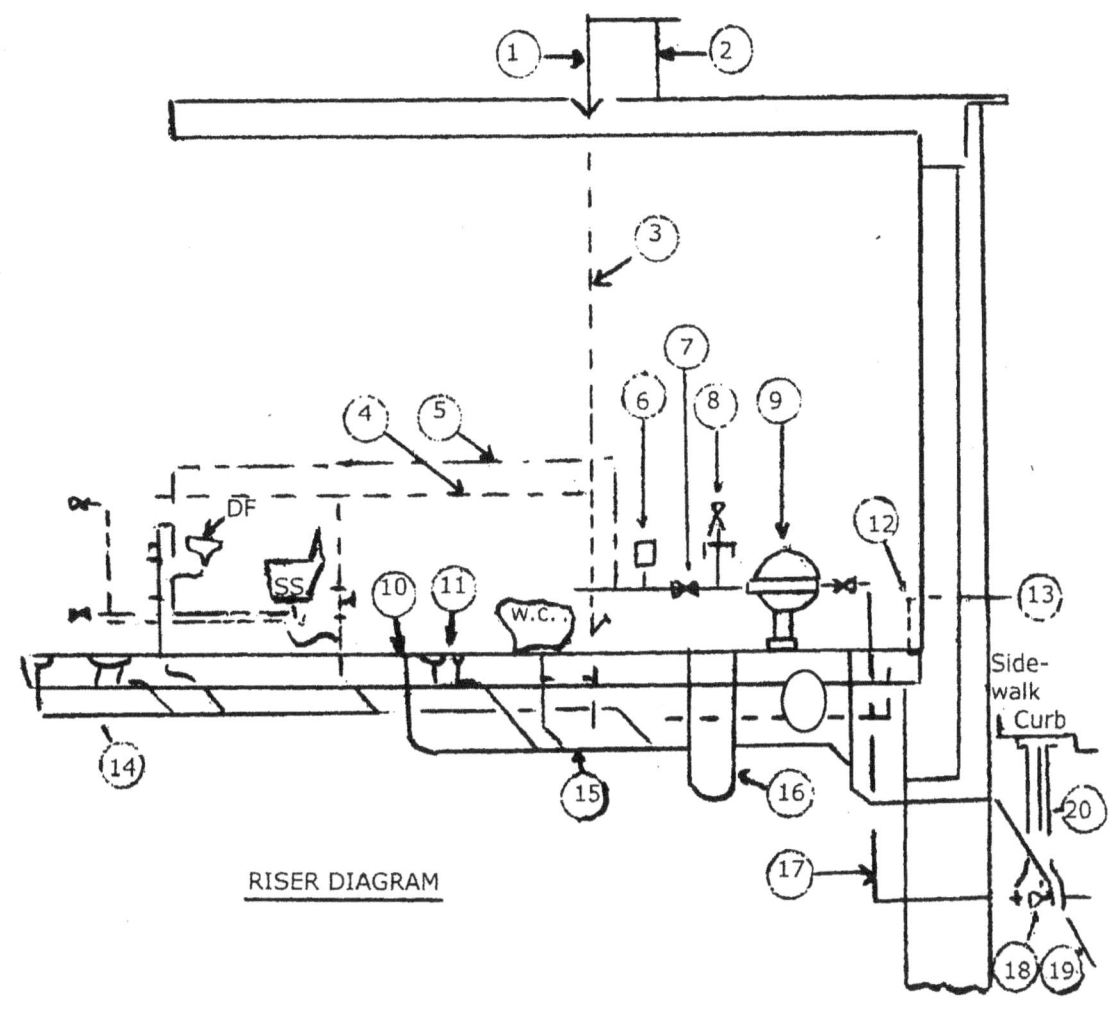

RISER DIAGRAM

44. According to the building code, the MINIMUM diameter of No. 1 and its minimum height, No. 2 respectively, are

    A. 2" and 12"   B. 3" and 18"
    C. 4" and 24"   D. 6" and 36"

44.____

45. No 6 is a

    A. relief valve   B. shock absorber
    C. testing connection   D. drain

45.____

46. No. 9 is a

    A. strainer   B. float valve
    C. meter   D. pedestal

46.____

47. No. 11 is a

    A. floor drain   B. cleanout
    C. trap   D. vent connection

47.____

48. No. 13 is a

    A. standpipe
    C. sprinkler head
    B. air inlet
    D. cleanout

49. The size of No. 16 is

    A. 2" x 2"
    C. 3" x 3"
    B. 2" x 3"
    D. 4" x 4"

50. No. 18 is a

    A. pressure reducing valve
    B. butterfly valve
    C. curb cock
    D. sprinkler head

KEY (CORRECT ANSWERS)

1. C	11. A	21. D	31. A	41. D
2. B	12. C	22. D	32. D	42. A
3. C	13. A	23. B	33. C	43. A
4. D	14. B	24. A	34. A	44. C
5. D	15. C	25. A	35. C	45. B
6. B	16. A	26. B	36. B	46. C
7. B	17. A	27. B	37. D	47. A
8. A	18. D	28. D	38. D	48. B
9. B	19. B	29. D	39. D	49. D
10. D	20. D	30. D	40. B	50. C

EXAMINATION SECTION
TEST 1

DIRECTIONS: Each question or incomplete statement is followed by several suggested answers or completions. Select the one that BEST answers the question or completes the statement. *PRINT THE LETTER OF THE CORRECT ANSWER IN THE SPACE AT THE RIGHT.*

1. The temperature at which water in an open vessel at sea level will boil is MOST NEARLY 1.____

   A. 100° F   B. 180° F   C. 212° F   D. 300° F

2. The fraction 3/8, expressed as a decimal, is 2.____

   A. 0.250   B. 0.281   C. 0.375   D. 0.406

3. The process of removing water, dissolved solids, and sludge from a boiler is called 3.____

   A. blowing down   B. screening
   C. topping   D. feeding

4. The remote control switch for all of the oil burners in a boiler room should be located 4.____

   A. adjacent to the boiler
   B. at each entrance to the boiler room
   C. on the mezzanine of the boiler room
   D. on the side of the boiler nearest an exit door

5. Of the following, an electrical fire should be extinguished with a fire extinguisher containing 5.____

   A. carbon tetrachloride   B. foamite
   C. carbon dioxide   D. soda acid

6. A steam preheater is COMMONLY used to 6.____

   A. generate superheated steam
   B. heat boiler make-up water
   C. heat #6 fuel oil before burning
   D. heat atmospheric air prior to combustion

7. Atomization as it applies to boiler operation is the process of 7.____

   A. breaking up atoms to obtain nuclear energy
   B. breaking up fuel oil into fine particles
   C. vaporizing water into steam
   D. mixing air and steam

8. The purpose of the try-cocks on a boiler is PRIMARILY to 8.____

   A. drain water from the boiler
   B. check the gage glass reading
   C. drain water from the gage glass
   D. blow down the boiler

9. A receiver in a compressed air system is used PRIMARILY to

   A. cool the air
   B. store the air
   C. remove particles of dust from the air
   D. saturate the air with vapor

10. A gage that can be used to measure either positive pressure or vacuum is GENERALLY called a _____ gage.

    A. pump   B. sight   C. compound   D. steam

11. With respect to heating systems, the MAIN purpose of using a thermostat in a room is to

    A. improve the efficiency of the oil burner
    B. increase the flow of heated air
    C. regulate the humidity
    D. regulate the temperature

12. An inter-cooler is a device USUALLY used on a

    A. refrigerator
    B. rotary gear pump
    C. centrifugal pump
    D. multistage air compressor

13. A boiler feed water regulator automatically regulates the _____ the boiler.

    A. supply of make-up water to
    B. temperature of the water being supplied to
    C. maximum water temperature in
    D. pressure of the water being supplied to

14. In the electrical trade, the term BX refers to

    A. amplifier hook-up wires
    B. insulated wires in a rigid conduit
    C. a cable consisting of insulated wires in a flexible metal tubing
    D. a cable consisting of insulated wires in a plastic outer covering

15. When threading pipe, the tool that holds the die is called a

    A. holder   B. stock   C. yawl   D. wedge

16. The PROPER tool to use to remove the burrs from the inside of a pipe is a

    A. chisel   B. file   C. cutter   D. reamer

17. The wrench which is MOST often used to make connections in the piping for a boiler is a

    A. pump pliers   B. gas pliers
    C. Stillson wrench   D. vise-grip pliers

18. If the combustion sensing device (lead sulphide cell) in a boiler installation does not *see* a flame, the boiler is automatically shut down by the closing of the

   A. breech damper
   B. magnetic oil valve
   C. primary air supply damper
   D. secondary air supply damper

19. A wrench that is COMMONLY used to tighten a nut where only a short swing of the wrench handle is possible is called a(n) _____ wrench.

   A. Stillson   B. monkey   C. ratchet   D. allen

20. A solenoid valve is GENERALLY operated by

   A. water temperature   B. water pressure
   C. electricity   D. oil pressure

21. The water hammer noise that is sometimes heard in the steam lines of a heating system is USUALLY caused by

   A. high steam pressure
   B. condensation in the steam
   C. impurities in the boiler water
   D. high flue gas temperatures

22. A sump system in a building is NORMALLY used to collect all boiler room waste water and move it into the house

   A. transfer pump   B. settling tank
   C. sewer   D. recirculation tank

23. A centrifugal pump is located above a sump pit. The type of valve that is installed on the end of the suction line to the pump to assure that the line is primed is called a _____ valve.

   A. needle   B. gate   C. globe   D. foot

24. A gag or clamp on a safety valve is GENERALLY used when

   A. making a hydrostatic test on a boiler
   B. testing the setting of the safety valve
   C. filling the boiler with water
   D. testing the quality of the water

25. The PRIME function of an electrical circuit breaker is similar to that of a

   A. capacitor   B. conductance
   C. switch   D. fuse

26. A valve that opens when a solenoid is energized and closes when it is de-energized is called a _____ valve.

   A. thermistor   B. magnetic
   C. thermostatic   D. pressure regulator

27. The device which stops the flow of fuel oil to an oil burner in case of primary air failure is GENERALLY known as a

    A. thermostat
    B. vaporstat
    C. pressuretrol
    D. low pressure cut-off

28. A device that is used to start the operation of high voltage electrical equipment by means of a low voltage control circuit is called a

    A. relay
    B. Wheatstone bridge
    C. Hartley circuit
    D. thermocouple

29. A pyrometer can be used to measure the

    A. temperature of flue gas
    B. pressure of fuel oil
    C. percentage of CO_2 in flue gas
    D. amount of soot in flue gas

30. The low water cut-off in a boiler is USUALLY controlled by means of a

    A. bimetallic strip
    B. float
    C. relay
    D. bellows

31. The type of pump COMMONLY used to pump No. 6 fuel oil from the storage oil tanks is a(n) _____ pump.

    A. centrifugal
    B. reciprocating
    C. gear
    D. axial

32. One of the uses of a pressuretrol on a fuel oil fired steam boiler is to

    A. control the water pressure so that it is equal to the steam pressure
    B. prevent the steam pressure from exceeding a set value
    C. control the pressure of the fuel oil so that it does not exceed the relief valve setting
    D. control the pressure of the condensate to the vacuum pump

33. The GREATEST safety hazard of storing oily rags is that they can

    A. cause a fire
    B. cause a foul odor
    C. produce toxic fumes
    D. attract vermin

34. Of the following, the BEST action to take if you find a small puddle of oil on the boiler room floor is to

    A. ignore it
    B. mop it up
    C. tell your supervisor
    D. cover it with sawdust

35. When a long ladder is placed against a high wall, a rope should be tied from the lowest rung to the wall.
    This is done to prevent

    A. anyone from walking under the ladder
    B. the ladder from slipping
    C. the rungs of the ladder from breaking
    D. someone from removing the ladder

36. Your fellow worker lifts one end of a piece of heavy equipment with a crowbar to permit you to work under this equipment with your hands.
    The PROPER safe procedure that you should follow is to

    A. insert temporary support blocks
    B. complete the job rapidly
    C. use heavy leather gloves
    D. lash the handle of the crowbar

37. Regulations require that domestic hot water should be supplied between the hours of

    A. 6:00 A.M. to 6:00 P.M.
    B. 6:00 A.M. to 12:00 Midnight
    C. 8:00 A.M. to 10:00 P.M.
    D. 12:00 Noon to 12:00 Midnight

38. In a fire tube boiler, it is MOST important to remove the soot from the

    A. outside surface of the tubes
    B. inside surface of the tubes
    C. walls of the combustion chamber
    D. intermediate tube sheet

39. A steam heating boiler is classified as a low pressure boiler when it generates steam at a gage pressure

    A. between 50 and 70 pounds per square inch
    B. between 30 and 50 pounds per square inch
    C. of 30 pounds per square inch or less
    D. of 15 pounds per square inch or less

40. The safety valve which is found on a steam boiler is designed to prevent the _____ from becoming too high.

    A. stack temperature
    B. water level
    C. steam pressure
    D. oil supply pressure

KEY (CORRECT ANSWERS)

1. C	11. D	21. B	31. C
2. C	12. D	22. C	32. B
3. A	13. A	23. D	33. A
4. B	14. C	24. A	34. B
5. C	15. B	25. D	35. B
6. C	16. D	26. B	36. A
7. B	17. C	27. B	37. B
8. B	18. B	28. A	38. B
9. B	19. C	29. A	39. D
10. C	20. C	30. B	40. C

TEST 2

DIRECTIONS: Each question or incomplete statement is followed by several suggested answers or completions. Select the one that BEST answers the question or completes the statement. *PRINT THE LETTER OF THE CORRECT ANSWER IN THE SPACE AT THE RIGHT.*

1. From the standpoint of corrosion resistance and reliability, the PREFERRED material for domestic hot water pipes from among the following is   1.___

    A. lead B. brass C. steel D. plastic

2. The packing which is GENERALLY found in the stuffing box of a centrifugal water pump is used to   2.___

    A. reduce bearing wear
    B. reduce noise
    C. prevent leakage of water
    D. compensate for shaft misalignment

3. The MAIN function of a steam trap is to   3.___

    A. remove condensate from a steam supply line
    B. restrict the flow of steam in a supply line
    C. filter dirt out of a condensate return line
    D. remove steam from a water line

4. The sum of 2'6", 0'3", and 3'1" is   4.___

    A. 2'9" B. 5'7" C. 5'10" D. 15'0"

5. A union is a plumbing fitting that is MOST commonly used to join   5.___

    A. two pieces of threaded pipe of the same diameter
    B. two pieces of threaded pipe of different diameter
    C. a gate valve to a threaded pipe
    D. an angle valve to a gate valve

6. A drain valve is used on a compressed air tank for the purpose of   6.___

    A. protecting the tank against excessively high pressures
    B. removing condensed vapor from the tank
    C. preventing air leakage from the tank
    D. starting the compressor

7. A valve which permits fluid to flow only in one direction in a pipe is called a _____ valve.   7.___

    A. needle B. gate C. globe D. check

8. The shade or color of the smoke emitted from burning fuel oil in a burner can be compared to a standard chart called a _____ chart.   8.___

    A. Neumann   B. Ringelmann
    C. Mann   D. Kirchoff

28

9. The three MOST important pollutants which come from burning fuel oil are: particulates, carbon monoxide, and   9._____

   A. oxygen
   B. carbon dioxide
   C. sulphur dioxide
   D. nitrogen

10. Number 6 fuel oil must be preheated before burning to   10._____

    A. reduce its viscosity
    B. increase its viscosity
    C. make use of excess steam
    D. make use of excess electricity

11. The deposits on the rotary oil cup of a burner should be cleaned with   11._____

    A. a file
    B. a metal scraper
    C. kerosene and a rag
    D. emery cloth

12. The low-water cut-off on a boiler should be tested by   12._____

    A. *lowering* the water level slowly
    B. *raising* the water level slowly
    C. *increasing* the firing rate
    D. *lowering* the firing rate

13. One POSSIBLE cause of smoke from an oil-fired boiler is   13._____

    A. contaminated boiler water
    B. low setting of the boiler relief valve
    C. low level of water in the boiler
    D. cold oil

14. The combustion efficiency of an oil-fired boiler can be determined from a combination of the _____ temperature and the percentage of _____ in the flue gas.   14._____

    A. flue gas; oxygen
    B. flue gas; carbon dioxide
    C. steam; oxygen
    D. steam; carbon monoxide

15. A relief valve is usually placed on the discharge side of the positive displacement fuel oil pump used to pump oil from the tank to the burner.   15._____
    The MAIN purpose of this relief valve is to

    A. increase the flow of oil to the burner
    B. increase the temperature of the fuel oil
    C. remove entrapped air
    D. protect the oil pump

16. To insure proper burning, the No. 6 fuel oil going to the oil burner is heated to a temperature that is MOST NEARLY   16._____

    A. 220° F   B. 180° F   C. 140° F   D. 100° F

17. The device that regulates the amount of steam flowing through a fuel oil steam preheater is called a   17._____

A. fuel oil pressure valve
B. fuel oil volume flow meter
C. steam volume flow meter
D. steam temperature regulator valve

18. Of the following materials, the one that is considered to have the BEST heat insulation property for a given thickness is

    A. wood
    B. glass wool
    C. copper
    D. steel

19. The function of the modutrol motor on a boiler is to

    A. open and close the fuel oil metering valve at the oil burner
    B. open and close the flow of fuel oil to the fuel oil heater
    C. control the flow of fuel oil from the storage tank
    D. control the flow of gas to ignite the fuel

20. The ignition system for an oil burner that burns No. 6 oil NORMALLY consists of a transformer, insulated electrodes and a(n)

    A. magnetic gas valve
    B. oil valve
    C. thermometer
    D. flow meter

21. A combustion sensing device, such as a lead sulfide cell, will close the magnetic valve feeding oil to the burner if it does not see a flame in APPROXIMATELY _____ to _____ seconds.

    A. $1; 1\frac{1}{2}$
    B. 2; 4
    C. $4\frac{1}{2}; 6$
    D. 8; 16

22. Bimetallic elements are NORMALLY found in _____ devices.

    A. pressure control
    B. temperature control
    C. pressure relief
    D. water level control

23. The cold oil interlock which prevents the oil burner from starting if the oil is too cold for proper smoke-free operation is located in the

    A. oil tank
    B. oil burner
    C. oil pump
    D. electric oil heater

24. The air flow interlock which will prevent the fuel oil valve from opening if there is no air pressure is located

    A. in the oil cup
    B. on top of the fan casing
    C. in the flue stack
    D. in the combustion chamber

25. A dirty or damaged oil cup in a rotary cup burner is MOST likely to cause

    A. poor mixing of oil and air
    B. an increase in oil flow
    C. an increase in oil pressure
    D. a decrease in air flow

26. The burner and boiler should each be inspected, cleaned, and overhauled _____ year(s).

    A. at least once a
    B. once every two
    C. once every three
    D. once every five

27. The accuracy of a fuel oil tank capacity gage is checked with a

    A. weighing scale
    B. pressure gage
    C. density meter
    D. dip stick

28. Vacuum tubes in oil burner control devices must be replaced even if they are in operating condition once every _____ months.

    A. 3
    B. 6
    C. 12
    D. 18

29. The soot blower used to blow soot out of the boiler tubes must be operated ONLY

    A. when the oil burner is shut down for at least 30 minutes
    B. when the oil burner is in operation
    C. when the oil burner is removed
    D. prior to operation of the burner

30. The pipe that leads from the storage oil tank to the outside of the building and which is at least 2 feet above the curb line and open to the atmosphere is called a _____ line.

    A. vent
    B. fill
    C. oil depth check
    D. suction

31. The device used to regulate draft in a furnace is called a

    A. damper
    B. stay bolt
    C. bonnet
    D. mudring

32. The secondary air damper is located under the burner, and the APPROXIMATE percentage of the total air that this damper supplies for complete fuel combustion is

    A. 30%
    B. 45%
    C. 70%
    D. 85%

33. The color that is MOST commonly used to identify a fire standpipe is

    A. bright red
    B. black
    C. bright blue
    D. silver gray

34. The device that starts and stops the sump pump at predetermined water levels in the sump pit is called a _____ switch.

    A. float
    B. micro
    C. double pole
    D. single pole

Questions 35-40.

DIRECTIONS: Questions 35 through 40, inclusive, are based on the paragraph *Hot Water Generation* shown below. When answering these questions, refer ONLY to this paragraph.

HOT WATER GENERATION

The hot water that comes from a faucet is called Domestic Hot Water.

It is heated by a steam coil that runs through a storage tank full of water in the basement of each building.

As the tenants take the hot water, fresh cold water enters the tank and is heated. The temperature of this water is automatically kept at approximately 140° F.

The device which controls the temperature is called a temperature regulator valve. It is operated by a bellows, capillary tube, and thermo bulb which connects between the valve and the hot water being stored in the tank. This bulb, tube, and bellows contains a liquid which expands and contracts with changes in temperature.

As the water in the tank reaches 140° F, the liquid in the thermo bulb expands and causes pressure to travel along the capillary tube and into the bellows. The expanded liquid forces the bellows to push the Temperature Regulator Valve Stem down, closing the valve. No more steam can enter the coil in the tank, and the water will get no hotter.

As the hot water is used by the tenants, cold water enters the tank and pulls the temperature down. This causes the liquid in the thermo bulb to cool and contract (shrink). The pressure is no longer in the bellows and a spring pushes it up, allowing the valve to open and allowing steam to again enter the heating coil in the storage tank raising the temperature of the Domestic Hot Water to 140° F.

35. Domestic hot water is heated by

   A. coal
   B. electricity
   C. hot water
   D. steam

36. The temperature of domestic hot water is MOST NEARLY

   A. 75° F   B. 100° F   C. 140° F   D. 212° F

37. The temperature of the hot water is controlled by a

   A. thermometer
   B. temperature regulator valve
   C. pressuretrol
   D. pressure gauge

38. The temperature regulator valve is operated by a combination of a

   A. thermometer and a thermo bulb
   B. thermometer and a pyrometer
   C. bellows, capillary tube, and a thermometer
   D. bellows, capillary tube, and a thermo bulb

39. Closing of the temperature regulator valve prevents _____ from entering the heating coil in the tank.

   A. water
   B. steam
   C. electricity
   D. air

40. As hot water is used by the tenants, the temperature of the water in the tank   40.____

    A. increases
    B. decreases
    C. remains the same
    D. approaches 212° F

KEY (CORRECT ANSWERS)

1. B	11. C	21. B	31. A
2. C	12. A	22. B	32. D
3. A	13. D	23. D	33. A
4. C	14. B	24. B	34. A
5. A	15. D	25. A	35. D
6. B	16. B	26. A	36. C
7. D	17. D	27. D	37. B
8. B	18. B	28. C	38. D
9. C	19. A	29. B	39. B
10. A	20. A	30. A	40. B

EXAMINATION SECTION
TEST 1

DIRECTIONS: Each question or incomplete statement is followed by several suggested answers or completions. Select the one that BEST answers the question or completes the statement. *PRINT THE LETTER OF THE CORRECT ANSWER IN THE SPACE AT THE RIGHT.*

1. Of the following classifications of fuel oils, the one which is NO longer made is   1.____

   A. #1   B. #2   C. #3   D. #6

2. Water at sea level and atmospheric pressure in an open container will boil at a temperature of   2.____

   A. 238° F   B. 212° F   C. 190° F   D. 172° F

3. A gauge pressure of 6.1 psi is equivalent to an absolute pressure of MOST NEARLY _____ psia.   3.____

   A. 30   B. 26   C. 21   D. 16

4. A pyrometer is used to measure   4.____

   A. draft   B. resistance
   C. temperature   D. velocity

5. Furnace draft is USUALLY measured in   5.____

   A. cubic feet   B. feet of mercury
   C. inches of air   D. inches of water

6. An ORSAT apparatus is used in a boiler plant to analyze   6.____

   A. feedwater   B. flue gas
   C. fuel   D. smoke haze

7. The device that prevents explosions in oil-fired boilers due to flame failure is the   7.____

   A. mercury tube   B. light sensing unit
   C. electrical transformer D. limit switch

8. The water level in a boiler operating 24 hours a day should be checked   8.____

   A. every 8 hours   B. once every 16 hours
   C. weekly   D. once every month

9. The boiler and oil burner should be inspected, overhauled, and cleaned at least once every   9.____

   A. 3 years   B. 18 months
   C. year   D. month

10. The PROPER procedure to follow when taking a boiler out of service is to   10.____

    A. *reduce* the fuel feed and slowly decrease the output
    B. *increase* the fuel feed and open all dampers

35

C. *open* all water supply valves and drain the boiler
D. *increase* the steam pressure and burn all the fuel

11. In the city, health regulations require domestic hot water to be supplied to tenants only between the hours of

    A. 6:00 A.M. to 12:00 Midnight
    B. 8:00 A.M. to 8:00 P.M.
    C. 12:00 Noon to 12:00 Midnight
    D. 10:00 A.M. to 6:00 P.M.

12. In an efficiently operated heating plant, the flue gas temperature should be APPROXIMATELY

    A. 150° F   B. 200° F   C. 350° F   D. 800° F

13. For MAXIMUM heat efficiency in a fire tube boiler, soot must be removed from the

    A. lifting rings
    B. outer tube surfaces
    C. walls of the crown sheet
    D. inner surface of the tubes

14. The percentage of carbon dioxide in the flue gas of an efficiently operated boiler should be APPROXIMATELY

    A. 4%   B. 6%   C. 12%   D. 18%

15. The combustion efficiency of a boiler is indicated by the amount of carbon dioxide in the flue gas and the

    A. size of the stack
    B. quality of the fuel
    C. temperature of the combustion air
    D. temperature of the flue gas

16. The pH value of boiler feedwater is normally MOST NEARLY kept at

    A. 3   B. 6   C. 10   D. 13

17. The one of the following that is used in the internal treatment of boiler feedwater to increase alkalinity is

    A. oxygen   B. tannin
    C. sodium alginate   D. soda ash

18. Of the following types of pumps, the one that is MOST commonly used with gun-type oil burners is the

    A. external or internal gear pump
    B. volute type
    C. centrifugal type
    D. propeller type

19. The hole in a direct-contact fire-actuated plug as used in a boiler is USUALLY filled with   19.____

    A. brass   B. lead   C. carbon   D. tin

20. The MAIN reason why soot blowers must be used only when the oil burners are in operation is to   20.____

    A. prevent a possible explosion
    B. reduce air pollution
    C. maintain building temperatures
    D. increase the boiler water temperature

21. The boiler low water cut-off is controlled by a   21.____

    A. relay   B. float   C. diaphragm   D. spring

22. The boiler connection from the last pass to the breech is called the   22.____

    A. drypan   B. rear tube
    C. safety outlet   D. bonnet

23. The function of a condensation pump in a steam system is to   23.____

    A. direct condensate to the house sewer
    B. prime the boiler
    C. condense steam to water
    D. return hot condensate to the boiler

24. A steam heating system that operates under both vacuum and low pressure conditions without the use of a vacuum pump is called a(n) _____ system.   24.____

    A. air   B. vapor   C. vacuum   D. water

25. A hot water heating boiler is classified as a low pressure boiler when it makes hot water at a gauge pressure NOT more than _____ psi.   25.____

    A. 300   B. 260   C. 200   D. 160

26. The one of the following gauge pressures that is MOST characteristic of a low pressure steam boiler is _____ psi.   26.____

    A. 30   B. 25   C. 20   D. 10

27. In the event of low water in a boiler, the burner will be shut down by the   27.____

    A. ignition transformer
    B. low water cut-off
    C. centrifugal switch on the burner
    D. damper control

28. A fuel oil steam preheater is USUALLY equipped with a   28.____

    A. mudring device
    B. steam temperature regulating valve
    C. steam volume gage
    D. boiler water level indicator

29. The MAIN function of a steam trap in a boiler heating system is to

   A. collect sediment from the steam lines
   B. return heat from the hot water to the building
   C. lower the temperature of the steam
   D. collect the water of condensation from steam apparatus

30. The one of the following which is a device that prevents the steam pressure in an oil-fired boiler from rising above a specified value is the

   A. pressuretrol   B. magnetic oil valve
   C. haze gauge   D. vaporstat

31. The type of valve used in feedwater lines where flow in only one direction is required is

   A. stop   B. gate   C. plug   D. check

32. The device that is used to force water into a boiler operating under pressure is the

   A. duplex   B. slide valve
   C. rocker arm   D. injector

33. The function of a feedwater heater in a boiler plant is to

   A. generate hot water for the building
   B. regulate the hot water temperature
   C. heat and condition water for the boiler
   D. condition chemicals for water leaving the boiler

34. A hot water heating system has an expansion tank to compensate for changes in the

   A. volume of water in the system
   B. volume of steam in the system
   C. water treatment process
   D. piping runs due to expansion of the metal pipe

35. One gallon of potable water weighs APPROXIMATELY _____ lbs.

   A. 6.8   B. 7.5   C. 8.3   D. 9.6

36. The bridge wall in a heating boiler is located

   A. above the arch
   B. in the steam drum
   C. behind the grates
   D. at the base of the chimney

37. A clamp or gag on a safety valve is generally used ONLY when

   A. testing a boiler hydrostatically
   B. surface-blowing the boiler
   C. adding chemicals to the feedwater
   D. cleaning the oil burner

38. Make-up water to a boiler is automatically controlled by the

    A. boiler water temperature
    B. boiler pressure
    C. metering valve
    D. feedwater regulator

39. Try-cocks are installed on a boiler for

    A. relieving air pressure in the system
    B. indicating the water level in the boiler
    C. blowing out the excess water from the boiler
    D. draining the water column

40. Steam preheaters are USUALLY used in an oil burning installation to

    A. preheat boiler feedwater
    B. add heat to saturated steam
    C. raise the temperature of the flue gas
    D. heat the fuel oil before it enters the burner

KEY (CORRECT ANSWERS)

1.	C	11.	A	21.	B	31.	D
2.	B	12.	C	22.	D	32.	D
3.	C	13.	D	23.	D	33.	C
4.	C	14.	C	24.	B	34.	A
5.	D	15.	D	25.	D	35.	C
6.	B	16.	C	26.	D	36.	C
7.	B	17.	D	27.	B	37.	A
8.	A	18.	A	28.	B	38.	D
9.	C	19.	D	29.	D	39.	B
10.	A	20.	A	30.	A	40.	D

TEST 2

DIRECTIONS: Each question or incomplete statement is followed by several suggested answers or completions. Select the one that BEST answers the question or completes the statement. *PRINT THE LETTER OF THE CORRECT ANSWER IN THE SPACE AT THE RIGHT.*

1. The temperature in a heated room can be regulated by a

    A. trap   B. scanner   C. damper   D. thermostat

2. Impurities and solids are removed from boiler water by a procedure known as

    A. screening   B. blowing down
    C. priming   D. foaming

3. To throttle the flow of steam in a steam line, use a

    A. brass mounting   B. gate valve
    C. globe valve   D. union

4. A highly objectionable air pollutant of fuel oil is

    A. nitrogen   B. carbon   C. hydrogen   D. sulphur

5. The modutrol motor on an oil-fired boiler controls the

    A. primary air damper
    B. gas flow for ignition
    C. oil returning to the fuel tank
    D. safety gauge

6. The one of the following that stops the flow of oil to the spinning cup of a rotary cup oil burner is the

    A. metering valve   B. magnetic oil valve
    C. regulating valve   D. fan casing

7. The one of the following that stops the flow of fuel oil to a rotary cup oil burner in the event of primary air failure is the

    A. vaporstat   B. electrode
    C. primary air damper   D. gas stop valve

8. In a rotary cup oil burner, the breaking up of the fuel oil into fine droplets is known as

    A. aeration   B. vaporization
    C. atomization   D. injection

9. The one of the following devices that controls the fuel oil temperature leaving the oil heater is the

    A. oil interlock   B. strainer
    C. aquastat   D. suction valve

10. Of the following causes of smoke in oil-burning installations, the one which occurs MOST frequently is 10.____

    A. faulty atomization due to insufficient preheat
    B. insufficient draft loss through the boiler
    C. insufficient air due to lack of draft
    D. too much oil being fed into a cold furnace on starting

11. The stack switch shuts off the oil to an oil burner in the event of 11.____

    A. an air pollution alert
    B. excessive boiler pressures
    C. on oversupply of fuel
    D. flame failure

12. In the city, the Ringelmann Chart is used to determine the density of 12.____

    A. smoke   B. coal   C. fuel oil   D. water

13. A centrifugal pump is MAINLY packed to 13.____

    A. prevent water leakage   B. lubricate the bearings
    C. reduce heat   D. prevent noise

14. The BEST procedure to follow when lubricating a pump is to apply lubricant 14.____

    A. only if needed
    B. on a regular schedule
    C. whenever you think the lubricant is low
    D. only when the pump is shut down

15. When pumping water out of a pit, the one of the following that should be installed on the suction end of the line is a 15.____

    A. foot valve   B. throttle valve
    C. volute   D. governor

16. The ASME Boiler Code is used for rating boilers. The letters ASME are an abbreviation for 16.____

    A. Allied for Standards of Mechanical Engineers
    B. American Society of Mechanical Engineers
    C. American Steam Maintenance Engineers
    D. American Society of Methods Engineers

17. The function of a sump pump in a boiler room is to collect boiler room drips and discharge it into the 17.____

    A. transfer tank   B. nearest public street
    C. conditioning tank   D. house sewer

18. Of the following instruments, the one that is used to measure atmospheric pressure is a(n) 18.____

    A. odometer   B. thermometer
    C. barometer   D. manometer

19. A compound gauge measures

    A. humidity and vacuum B. temperature and pressure
    C. pressure and vibration D. pressure and vacuum

20. An inter-cooler would GENERALLY be installed on a(n)

    A. air compressor B. rotary gear pump
    C. fuel tank D. evaporator

21. The one of the following that is BEST to use to loosen a rusted bolt is

    A. penetrating oil B. engine oil
    C. graphite D. silica

22. The one of the following that is used to thread a pipe externally is called a

    A. guide B. die C. stock D. tap

23. A frequent cause of knocking in low-pressure steam lines is

    A. condensation of the steam
    B. an increase of steam temperature
    C. high water temperature
    D. insufficient fuel supply

24. Viscosity is a measure of the resistance of a fuel oil to

    A. burning B. flowing
    C. vaporization D. deterioration

25. The PROPER procedure to follow for safety when working on a ladder is to

    A. not face the ladder when descending
    B. use a sturdy object to obtain additional ladder height
    C. take one step at a time when ascending or descending a ladder
    D. always have two men on the ladder at the same time

26. Oily waste rags should be kept in a closed metal container MAINLY to

    A. prevent fire
    B. keep the rags from drying out
    C. eliminate attraction to bugs
    D. prevent oil seepage onto the floor

27. Fire standpipe systems are GENERALLY painted

    A. black B. red C. blue D. white

28. The oil burner remote control switch should be located

    A. on the front of the boiler
    B. on the stack of the boiler
    C. at the control panel
    D. at each entrance to the boiler room

29. Insulated electrical wire in flexible metal tubing is known as

    A. BX   B. cable   C. RX   D. conduit

30. The one of the following that is used to measure air pressure is a

    A. calorimeter   B. venturi
    C. compensator   D. manometer

31. Pressures below atmospheric are USUALLY expressed in

    A. pounds of air   B. inches of water
    C. inches of mercury   D. pounds of steam

32. The reading of the fuel oil tank capacity gauge is checked by using a

    A. steam nozzle   B. dip stick
    C. drip pan   D. pressure gauge

33. In piping systems, nominal size refers to

    A. outside diameter   B. length in feet
    C. inside diameter   D. weight in pounds

34. The one of the following plumbing fittings which is used to connect two pieces of the same diameter threaded pipe is a

    A. cap   B. bushing   C. union   D. plug

35. A four-inch-long galvanized pipe having a diameter of one inch and male threads at both ends is called a(n)

    A. nipple   B. turnbuckle
    C. elbow   D. coupling

36. A galvanized flue pipe with an outside diameter of seven inches will have a circumference in inches of MOST NEARLY equal to

    A. 22   B. 20   C. 19   D. 17

37. The sum of 2.6", 1.2", and 4.1" is

    A. 6.6"   B. 7.3"   C. 7.9"   D. 8.2"

38. An electric motor is NORMALLY rated in

    A. ohms   B. farads
    C. horsepower   D. megawatts

39. The one of the following electrical devices which USUALLY contains a magnetic coil is the

    A. battery   B. thermocouple
    C. relay   D. fustat

40. The MOST important requirement of a good boiler room report is that it should be 40.___
    A. prepared quickly
    B. short and clear
    C. very long and detailed
    D. shown to the building tenants

KEY (CORRECT ANSWERS)

1. D	11. D	21. A	31. C
2. B	12. A	22. B	32. B
3. C	13. A	23. A	33. A
4. D	14. B	24. B	34. C
5. A	15. A	25. C	35. A
6. B	16. B	26. A	36. A
7. A	17. D	27. B	37. C
8. C	18. C	28. D	38. C
9. C	19. D	29. A	39. C
10. D	20. A	30. D	40. B

EXAMINATION SECTION
TEST 1

DIRECTIONS: Each question or incomplete statement is followed by several suggested answers or completions. Select the one that BEST answers the question or completes the statement. *PRINT THE LETTER OF THE CORRECT ANSWER IN THE SPACE AT THE RIGHT.*

1. An instrument that is USUALLY mounted on a boiler control panel and which is read in inches of water is known as a(n) _____ gauge.

    A. pressure
    B. draft
    C. stack temperature
    D. Orsat indicator

    1._____

2. The type of pump which SHOULD be used to supply fuel oil to a low pressure boiler is the _____ pump.

    A. centrifugal
    B. diaphragm
    C. rotary gear
    D. reciprocating

    2._____

3. A thermostatic radiator trap which is working satisfactorily will

    A. *open* to pass the steam
    B. *open* to pass the condensate
    C. *close* to retain the cool air
    D. *close* to retain the condensate

    3._____

4. Readings of stack temperature and percentage of carbon dioxide are USEFUL in the boiler room in determining changes in the boiler's _____ efficiency.

    A. mechanical
    B. volumetric
    C. overall
    D. combustion

    4._____

5. In the start-up cycle of a boiler which is equipped with all of the following devices, the device that should be energized BEFORE all the others is the

    A. magnetic oil valve
    B. ignition transformer
    C. gas solenoid valve
    D. fresh air louvre motor

    5._____

6. The one of the following valves which is electrically operated is the _____ valve.

    A. pressure relief
    B. magnetic oil
    C. check
    D. thermostatic control

    6._____

7. In an installation where there is only one fuel oil pump set, a duplex strainer is PREFERABLY used because

    A. one side of the strainer can be cleaned without interrupting the flow of oil
    B. one side of the strainer will screen out much finer particles than the other side
    C. the flow of oil can be directed through both sides at the same time, thereby increasing the velocity of the oil
    D. cleaning of a duplex strainer is not required during the heating season

    7._____

8. A higher-than-normal vacuum reading on a gauge which is attached to the suction side of a fuel oil pump GENERALLY indicates that there is

    8._____

A. no oil in the tank
B. a clogged strainer in the suction line
C. a broken fitting in the suction line
D. worn packing on the pump

9. The one of the following which is NOT a possible point of entry of water leaking into the fuel oil storage tank is the

   A. fuel fill pipe can
   B. sounding well plug
   C. steam coil in a fuel oil heater
   D. fire box side of the furnace wall

10. When an air vaporstat which is connected to an automatic rotary cup oil burner senses the loss of primary air pressure in the fan housing, it DE-ENERGIZES the

    A. burner motor-starter coil
    B. magnetic oil valve
    C. secondary air damper control
    D. modutrol motor

11. A steam boiler which is externally fired and in which the hot gases pass through the tubes is COMMONLY known as a _____ boiler.

    A. scotch
    B. locomotive
    C. horizontal return tubular
    D. vertical tubular

12. The modulating pressuretrol on an automatic rotary cup oil-fired boiler controls the

    A. modutrol motor circuit   B. magnetic oil valve
    C. burner motor starter   D. electric heater

13. The reason for *blowing down* a boiler is to

    A. lower the boiler water level below the boiler tubes
    B. reduce the concentration of dissolved solids in the boiler water
    C. reduce the concentration of dissolved oxygen in the boiler water
    D. eliminate the need for treating the boiler water chemically

14. The one of the following boiler pressure-actuated devices which should be adjusted to operate at the HIGHEST pressure setting is the

    A. pop-safety valve   B. manual-reset pressuretrol
    C. modulating pressuretrol   D. limit pressuretrol

15. The BEST procedure for testing the operation of a low-water cutout is to lower the _____ until the burner shuts off.

    A. boiler water level rapidly
    B. boiler water level slowly
    C. water level in the water column rapidly
    D. water level in the water column slowly

16. If the water disappears from the gauge glass on a low-pressure oil-fired boiler, the FIRST action the boiler operator should take is to

    A. shut off the water
    B. add water to the boiler until the glass fills up to the correct level
    C. open the bottom blow-down valve
    D. blow down the water column

17. On a certain day, the lowest outside temperature was 20°F and the highest was 40°F. The number of degree days for this day is

    A. 25   B. 30   C. 35   D. 45

18. A vacuum return line pump should NOT be operated with the electrical control set for

    A. continuous operation
    B. float and vacuum control
    C. float control *only*
    D. vacuum control *only*

19. The PREFERRED location for a Dunham Selector is on the _____ exposure of the building.

    A. north   B. east   C. south   D. west

20. Maintaining a Dunham heat balancer in good working order requires annual cleaning of its

    A. radiator fins   B. relay contacts
    C. solenoid valve   D. fulcrum

21. An automatic device used for regulating air temperature is a(n)

    A. rheostat   B. aquastat   C. thermostat   D. duostat

22. Smoke alarms which must be installed on oil-fired boilers should create a loud signal and a red flashing light upon the emission of an air contaminant whose density, when compared to the standard smoke chart, appears DARKER than Number _____ on the chart.

    A. 1   B. 2   C. 3   D. 4

23. Samples for the testing of boiler water should be taken from the

    A. bottom blow-off   B. condensate tank
    C. water column   D. condensate return line

24. In a building which is heated by an oil-fired boiler, 2,100 gallons of fuel oil were burned in a period in which the degree days reached a total of 1,400.
    If all other conditions remained constant, the number of gallons of fuel oil that would be burned in this building during a period in which the degree days reached a total of 3,600 is

    A. 2,400   B. 2,900   C. 4,800   D. 5,400

25. Of the following fuels, the one with the HIGHEST viscosity is   25.____

    A. kerosene
    B. natural gas
    C. #6 oil
    D. #2 oil

KEY (CORRECT ANSWERS)

1.	B	11.	C
2.	C	12.	A
3.	B	13.	B
4.	D	14.	A
5.	D	15.	B
6.	B	16.	C
7.	A	17.	C
8.	B	18.	D
9.	D	19.	A
10.	B	20.	A

21. C
22. A
23. C
24. D
25. C

TEST 2

DIRECTIONS: Each question or incomplete statement is followed by several suggested answers or completions. Select the one that BEST answers the question or completes the statement. *PRINT THE LETTER OF THE CORRECT ANSWER IN THE SPACE AT THE RIGHT.*

1. An indicator card from a steam engine is MOST useful in   1.____

    A. determining the boiler pressure
    B. determining the engine speed
    C. adjusting the valve setting
    D. computing the mechanical efficiency

2. Which of the following statements is MOST NEARLY correct?   2.____

    A. A water tube boiler has the combustion gases inside the tubes.
    B. A scotch marine boiler has 2 drums.
    C. A brick set HRT boiler usually has a steel fire box.
    D. The circulation in a boiler may be either gravity or forced.

3. When the load on a mechanical stoker fired boiler plant furnishing steam for slide valve engine generators drops by 30%, the   3.____

    A. stoker should be shut down
    B. fan should be speeded up and the stoker slowed
    C. stoker should be speeded up and the air supply reduced
    D. stoker speed and air supply should be adjusted by reducing both

4. Which of the following statements is MOST NEARLY correct?   4.____

    A. All types of mechanical stokers may be used with equal efficiency under all types of boilers.
    B. Most stokers are designed with a weak member.
    C. The best type of stoker to use is not dependent upon the type of fuel available.
    D. The advisability of installing stokers is not dependent upon the load.

5. The number and size of safety valves required on a high pressure boiler is dependent upon the   5.____

    A. size of the boiler drums
    B. amount of heating surface
    C. number of pounds of fuel burned per square foot of grate per hour
    D. size of the steam main

6. In changing over a boiler from high pressure (150 lbs. per square inch) to 10 lbs. per square inch, it is usually NECESSARY to   6.____

    A. *increase* the size of the safety valves
    B. *decrease* the grate area
    C. *increase* the size of the feed water piping
    D. *increase* the size of the blow down piping

49

7. A boiler feed injector becomes temporarily steam bound. To correct this condition, the MOST proper action to take is to

   A. increase boiler pressure
   B. reduce suction lift
   C. wrap it with cold rags
   D. bank fire

8. The PROPER method of laying up a steam boiler for a period of less than one month is to

   A. drain all the water and let the boiler dry out
   B. fill it with treated water to the top of the tubes
   C. fill it with treated water to the stop valve
   D. fill it with treated water to the level of the upper try cock

9. In the winter time, heating complaints by tenants should be investigated

   A. only if there are several complaints from one building
   B. only if the outside temperature is below 40°F
   C. immediately
   D. by the assistant superintendent

10. Compared to the input of the electric ignition transformer associated with #6 oil burners, the output is _____ voltage, _____ current.

    A. higher; higher
    B. higher; lower
    C. lower; higher
    D. lower; lower

11. A pressure regulator valve in a compressed air line should be

    A. preceded by a water and oil separator
    B. preceded by a solenoid valve
    C. followed by a water and oil separator
    D. followed by a solenoid valve

12. A preventive maintenance program in a boiler room should provide for the routine periodic replacement of

    A. badly leaking boiler tubes
    B. electric motors
    C. safety valve springs
    D. programmer electronic tubes

13. Steam heated hot water tank coils can be tested for leaks by

    A. chemically testing the domestic hot water leaving the tank
    B. chemically testing the condensate leaving the coil
    C. pressure testing the domestic water in the tank
    D. pressure testing the condensate return

14. The chemical which is added to boiler water to reduce its oxygen content is sodium

    A. carbonate   B. chloride   C. alginate   D. sulphite

15. Wear in the sleeve bearings of an electric motor is MOST likely to result in a change in the

   A. pole spacing
   B. armature balance
   C. air gap
   D. line frequency

16. Assume that only the first few coils of a hot water convector used for heating a room are hot.
   To correct this, you should FIRST

   A. increase the water pressure
   B. increase the water temperature
   C. bleed the air out of the convector
   D. clean the convector pipes

17. When priming occurs in a boiler,

   A. the fire will be extinguished
   B. the steam becomes superheated and too dry
   C. the fire tubes become overheated and may crack
   D. water particles are carried over with the steam into the steam lines

18. One of the ways to prevent or reduce the amount of smoke from a furnace is to

   A. reduce the quantity of air supplied to the fire box
   B. supply coal in large quantities and no more than twice a day
   C. cool the fire bed to prevent high temperatures in the fire box
   D. keep live coals at the top of the fire bed

19. Of the following, the SMALLEST size coal is

   A. chestnut   B. egg   C. buckwheat   D. pea

20. If coal is to be stored, the following precaution should be followed:

   A. Coal should be piled in conical piles rather than horizontal layers
   B. Coal should be placed in storage on hot summer days
   C. Avoid alternate wetting and drying of coal
   D. Coal should be piled no more than three feet deep

21. The HRT boiler contains

   A. fire tubes in which hot gases flow
   B. water tubes in which water flows to form steam
   C. no horizontal return tubes
   D. no way in which a vacuum return can be connected

22. A room is properly heated in the winter time when the temperature is about _____ °F and the relative humidity is _____%.

   A. 70; 40 to 60
   B. 78; 40 to 60
   C. 65; 30
   D. 75; 90

23. The average temperature on a day in January is 30°F. This would be called a _____ degree day.

    A. 40   B. 35   C. 30   D. 25

24. The term BTU is used in connection with

    A. heating quality of a fuel
    B. the size of boiler tubes
    C. radiator fittings
    D. heating qualities of radiators

25. Which one of the following is NOT the cause of clinker formation?

    A. Poor quality coal
    B. Thick fires
    C. Closed ashpit doors
    D. Water sprayed into the ashpit at intervals during the day

KEY (CORRECT ANSWERS)

1.	C	11.	A
2.	D	12.	D
3.	D	13.	B
4.	B	14.	D
5.	B	15.	C
6.	A	16.	C
7.	C	17.	D
8.	C	18.	D
9.	C	19.	C
10.	B	20.	C

21.	A
22.	A
23.	B
24.	A
25.	D

TEST 3

DIRECTIONS: Each question or incomplete statement is followed by several suggested answers or completions. Select the one that BEST answers the question or completes the statement. *PRINT THE LETTER OF THE CORRECT ANSWER IN THE SPACE AT THE RIGHT.*

1. With steam at a temperature of 365°F in a boiler, which of the following stack gas temperatures would you consider to be good usual operating practice in a plant without economizers, air preheaters, and the like?   1.____

    A. 300°F B. 500°F C. 700°F D. 900°F

2. The percentage of CO_2 in the stack gases is an indication of the   2.____

    A. rate of combustion in the furnace
    B. rate at which excess air is supplied to the furnace
    C. rate of carbon monoxide production in the furnace
    D. temperature of combustion

3. In the most usual type of large capacity oil burner using #6 oil, under *fully automatic* control, the atomization of the oil is produced MAINLY by the   3.____

    A. pressure from the pump
    B. pressure from the secondary air fan
    C. oil temperature from the heater
    D. rotation of the burner assembly by the motor

4. Of the following, the figure which comes the CLOSEST to indicating the number of degree days in a normal heating season in New York City is   4.____

    A. 3000 B. 4000 C. 5000 D. 6000

5. In which of the following methods of steam generation would you expect to obtain reasonably continuous values of CO_2 CLOSEST to the perfect CO_2 value?   5.____
Automatic

    A. stoker firing with temperature recorder
    B. stoker firing with *hold five timer*
    C. oil firing with *stack switch*
    D. oil firing with *haze regulator*

6. The loss of heat in stack gases for heavy fuel oil is
HIGHEST when the CO_2 content is _____% and the stack temperature is _____°   6.____

    A. 12; 500 B. 8; 600 C. 6; 700 D. 14; 600

7. A badly sooted HRT boiler under coal firing will show a _____ than a clean boiler.   7.____

    A. higher CO_2 value
    B. lower CO_2 value
    C. higher stack temperature
    D. lower draft loss

8. A unit heater condensing 50 lbs. of low pressure steam per hour would be rated MOST NEARLY at _____ square feet E.D.R.

   A. 50 B. 100 C. 150 D. 200

9. One horsepower MOST NEARLY equals

   A. 550 ft.-lbs. per second
   B. 3300 ft.-lbs. per minute
   C. 55000 ft.-lbs. per hour
   D. 10000 ft.-lbs. per minute

10. A pressure gauge attached to a standpipe system shows a pressure of 36 pounds per square inch.
    The head of water, in feet, above the gauge is MOST NEARLY

    A. 24 B. 36 C. 60 D. 83

11. Of the following, the term *vapor barrier* would MOST likely be associated with

    A. electric service installation
    B. insulation materials
    C. fuel oil tank installation
    D. domestic gas piping

12. Pitot tubes are used to

    A. test feed water for impurities
    B. measure air or gas flow in a duct
    C. prevent overheating of elements of a steam gauge
    D. control the ignition system of an oil burner

13. In warm air heating and in ventilating systems, laboratories and kitchens should NOT be equipped with return ducts in order to

    A. keep air velocities in other returns as high as possible
    B. reduce fire hazards
    C. reduce the possibility of circulating odors through the system
    D. keep the temperature high in these rooms

14. One square foot of equivalent direct steam radiation (EDR) is equivalent to a heat emission of _____ BTU per _____.

    A. 150; hour   B. 240; minute
    C. 150; minute   D. 240; hour

15. Of the following, the one which is LEAST likely to cause continuous vibration of an operating motor is

    A. a faulty starting circuit
    B. excessive belt tension
    C. the misalignment of motor and driven equipment
    D. loose bearings

16. The function of a steam trap is to

    A. remove sediment and dirt from steam
    B. remove air and non-condensible gases from steam
    C. relieve excessive steam pressure to the atmosphere
    D. remove condensate from a pipe or an apparatus

17. The temperature at which air is just saturated with the moisture present in it is called its

    A. relative humidity
    B. absolute humidity
    C. humid temperature
    D. dew point

18. Of the following, the one which is NOT a general class of oil burners is the _____ atomizing.

    A. water
    B. rotary cup
    C. mechanical
    D. air

19. Of the following, the one which should be between a boiler and its safety valve is

    A. a swing check valve of a size larger than that of the safety valve
    B. a butterfly valve located in the boiler nozzle
    C. a gate valve of the same nominal size as that of the safety valve
    D. no valve of any type

20. The term *spinner cup* refers to

    A. screw-type stokers
    B. gun-type oil burners
    C. rotary-type oil burners
    D. chain grate stokers

21. A gun-type burner is often used on a

    A. pot-type oil burner
    B. low pressure gas boiler
    C. coal underfeed stoker boiler
    D. high pressure oil-fired boiler

22. Of the following, the action that should be taken as the FIRST step if a properly adjusted safety valve on a steam boiler *pops off* when in operation is

    A. open the draft
    B. add more water to the boiler
    C. wire the valve shut
    D. reduce the draft

23. When the water gets below the safe level in an operating boiler, it is BEST to

    A. add new water up to the safe level and open up the fire so that the water will heat quickly
    B. check the fire and let the boiler cool down before new water is added
    C. add new water to the boiler immediately
    D. check the fire and empty the boiler

24. Vents on fuel oil storage tanks are used to

   A. fill the fuel tanks
   B. allow air to escape during filling
   C. check oil flash points
   D. make tank fuel soundings

25. Of the following, the MOST desirable way to remove carbon deposits from the atomizing cup of an oil burner is to

   A. apply a hot flame to the carbonized surfaces to burn off the carbon deposits
   B. use kerosene to loosen the deposits and wipe with a soft cloth
   C. wash the cup with a mild trisodium phosphate solution and dry with a cloth
   D. use a scraper, followed by light rubbing with emery cloth

---

KEY (CORRECT ANSWERS)

1.	B	11.	B
2.	B	12.	B
3.	D	13.	C
4.	C	14.	D
5.	D	15.	A
6.	C	16.	D
7.	C	17.	D
8.	D	18.	A
9.	A	19.	D
10.	D	20.	C

21.	D
22.	D
23.	B
24.	B
25.	B

EXAMINATION SECTION
TEST 1

DIRECTIONS: Each question or incomplete statement is followed by several suggested answers or completions. Select the one that BEST answers the question or completes the statement. *PRINT THE LETTER OF THE CORRECT ANSWER IN THE SPACE AT THE RIGHT.*

1. The capacity of a water-cooled condenser is LEAST affected by the   1.____

    A. surrounding air temperature
    B. water temperature
    C. refrigerant temperature
    D. quantity of water being circulated

2. The type of refrigeration system MOST commonly used in ice-skating rinks is the _____ system.   2.____

    A. direct expansion   B. simple secondary
    C. compound secondary   D. quadric resistance

3. The theoretical amount of refrigeration required to freeze one ton of water from 66° F to ice at 28° F in one day is _____ ton(s).   3.____

    A. 1.00   B. 1.25   C. 1.50   D. 1.75

4. The brine solution MOST commonly used in ice-skating rink piping, as a freezing medium, is a mixture of water and   4.____

    A. calcium chloride   B. sodium chloride
    C. glycol   D. methanol

5. In an absorption refrigeration system, latent heat is absorbed by the refrigerant in the   5.____

    A. evaporator and the generator
    B. evaporator and the absorber
    C. condenser and the absorber
    D. condenser and the generator

6. Of the following refrigerants, the one which has the HIGHEST evaporator pressure at the standard 5° F temperature is   6.____

    A. ammonia   B. freon 12
    C. methyl-chloride   D. carbon dioxide

7. The cooler in a refrigeration system that is equipped with automatic protective devices is MOST likely to be accidentally damaged by water freeze-up when the   7.____

    A. system is operating under reduced load
    B. system is operating at rated load
    C. system is being pumped down
    D. condenser cooling water flow is interrupted

8. The one of the following statements pertaining to refrigerant compressor lubricants that is NOT true is that

   A. the type of oil that is used to lubricate centrifugal compressors can also be used in speed increasers
   B. ammonia causes very little viscosity change in lubricating oil
   C. most reciprocating compressors handling ammonia or freons can be lubricated properly with an oil having a viscosity of 300 Sec. SU @ 100° F
   D. freon 12 causes very little viscosity change in lubricating oil

9. The one of the following capacity controls which is USUALLY found in a refrigerant reciprocating-compressor system is a

   A. suction valve unloader
   B. throttling damper
   C. variable inlet guide vane
   D. condenser temperature control

10. A thermostatic expansion valve is connected to an evaporator operating at 5° F and 11.8 psig. The valve is in equilibrium at 10° superheat, and the pressure in the bulb is 17.7 psig.
    The EQUIVALENT valve-spring pressure on the refrigerant side of the sensitive element is _____ psi.

    A. 5.9   B. 10.9   C. 22.8   D. 29.5

11. A pressure gage on a compressed air tank reads 35.3 psi at 70° F.
    If, due to a fire, the temperature of the air in the tank were to increase to 600° F, the gage reading should be MOST NEARLY _____ psi.

    A. 70   B. 75   C. 80   D. 85

12. An ADVANTAGE that variable-speed control of a fan has over damper control is

    A. lower first-cost of controls
    B. lower power consumption
    C. cheaper fan drive motor
    D. constant high efficiency throughout entire fan load range

13. An intercooler is used on a two-stage air compressor to reduce the

    A. cylinder temperature in the first stage
    B. amount of condensate in the second stage
    C. back pressure of the air in the first stage
    D. work done on the air in the second stage

14. Of the following, the BEST instrument to use to measure small pressure differentials at low pressure is the

    A. mercury manometer   B. bourdon tube gage
    C. pressurtrol   D. inclined manometer

15. A modulating pressurtrol on a boiler should contain a

    A. potentiometer
    B. mercury switch
    C. manual reset lever
    D. level indicator

16. Of the following automatic refrigerant expansion valves, the one which can only be used in a system where the liquid refrigerant can largely be stored in the evaporator without danger of sending slugs of liquid refrigerant over to the compressor is the _____ valve.

    A. thermal-expansion
    B. diaphragm-expansion
    C. high-side float
    D. low-side float

17. The refrigerating effect of a fluid is measured by the amount of heat it is capable of absorbing from the time it enters the

    A. evaporator as a liquid and leaves as a vapor
    B. condenser as a vapor and leaves as a liquid
    C. expansion valve as a liquid and leaves as a vapor
    D. compressor as a vapor and leaves as a vapor

18. The one of the following which lists the refrigerants in CORRECT order of decreasing toxicity is:

    A. Ammonia, sulphur dioxide, freon 12
    B. Sulphur dioxide, ammonia, freon 12
    C. Sulphur dioxide, freon 12, ammonia
    D. Ammonia, freon 12, sulphur dioxide

19. The one of the following methods which would MOST likely be used to control the capacity of a large centrifugal refrigerant compressor is the _____ method.

    A. cylinder unloader
    B. variable cylinder clearance
    C. variable speed
    D. stop and start

20. On a hot summer day, the GREATEST number of people working in a large air-conditioned office would feel comfortable if the temperature and relative humidity were maintained at

    A. 77° F and 50%
    B. 80° F and 60%
    C. 74° F and 30%
    D. 71° F and 50%

21. The one of the following conditions which has the GREATEST effect on the suction pressure on a swimming pool circulating pump is a

    A. clogged hair and lint strainer
    B. loss of coagulant
    C. low pH level
    D. clogged filter

22. A coagulant used in swimming pool filters is

    A. alum
    B. chlorine
    C. soda-ash
    D. sodium hypochlorite

23. According to the health code, the pH reading of swimming pool water should be between _____ and _____.

    A. 5.8; 6.4   B. 6.8; 7.4   C. 7.8; 8.4   D. 8.8; 9.4

24. An orthotolidine test is made to find out how much of which substance is contained in a sample of water?

    A. Alum   B. Ammonia   C. Chlorine   D. Soda-ash

25. The MINIMUM air temperature which must be maintained in an indoor swimming pool, except during the summer months, is _____ °F.

    A. 68   B. 71   C. 75   D. 82

KEY (CORRECT ANSWERS)

1. A
2. B
3. B
4. A
5. A

6. D
7. C
8. D
9. A
10. A

11. D
12. B
13. D
14. D
15. A

16. C
17. A
18. B
19. C
20. A

21. A
22. A
23. C
24. C
25. C

TEST 2

DIRECTIONS: Each question or incomplete statement is followed by several suggested answers or completions. Select the one that BEST answers the question or completes the statement. *PRINT THE LETTER OF THE CORRECT ANSWER IN THE SPACE AT THE RIGHT.*

1. A permit is required for the storage or use of liquid chlorine. This permit is issued by which city agency? The

   A. Health Services Administration
   B. Board of Standards and Appeals
   C. Board of Water Supply
   D. Fire Department

2. The MINIMUM amount of free chlorine that swimming pool water should contain for proper disinfection is _____ part(s) per million.

   A. 1.0   B. 10   C. 40   D. 400

3. The agency which approves gas masks suitable for use in high concentrations of chlorine gas is the United States

   A. Environmental Protection Agency
   B. Department of Agriculture
   C. Bureau of Mines
   D. Department of Defense

4. The daily operational records of swimming pools which are required by the health code must be kept for a period of AT LEAST

   A. one month   B. six months
   C. one year   D. two years

5. The one of the following which is NOT used as a filtering media in swimming pool filters is

   A. sand   B. quartz
   C. diatomaceous earth   D. clay

6. The point at which swimming pool filters should be back-washed is when the difference between the inlet and outlet pressure EXCEEDS _____ psi.

   A. 5   B. 10   C. 15   D. 20

7. Of the following valves, the type which can be used to adjust the rate-of-flow in a swimming pool filter is the _____ valve.

   A. butterfly   B. needle
   C. gate   D. stop-and-waste

8. When the coagulant in a swimming pool filter fails to jelly, the MOST likely cause of the failure is

   A. high water temperature   B. excess bacteria in the water
   C. insufficient alkalinity of the water   D. excess algae in the water

61

9. Of the following types of flow meters, the one that is MOST accurate is a

   A. concentric orifice B. venturi tube
   C. flow nozzle   D. pitot tube

10. A spring pop safety valve on a fired high-pressure boiler fails to pop at its set pressure. Which of the following methods should be used to free the valve before retesting it?

    A. Strike the valve body with a soft lead hammer until it pops
    B. Raise the valve lifting-lever and release it
    C. Reduce the spring compression gradually until the valve opens
    D. Unscrew the valve one-quarter turn to relieve the strain on it

11. A device which retains the desired parts of a steam and water mixture while rejecting the undesired parts of the mixture is a

    A. check valve   B. calorimeter
    C. stud tube   D. steam trap

12. The PRIMARY purpose of using phosphate to treat boiler water is to

    A. precipitate the hardness constituents
    B. scavenge the dissolved oxygen
    C. dissolve the calcium
    D. dissolve the magnesium

13. The efficiency of a riveted joint is defined as the ratio of the

    A. plate thickness to the rivet diameter
    B. strength of the riveted joint to the strength of a welded joint
    C. strength of the riveted joint to the strength of the solid plate
    D. number of rivets in the first row of the joint to the total number of rivets on one side of the joint

14. A pump delivers 1500 pounds of water per minute against a total head of 200 feet. The water horsepower of this pump is MOST NEARLY

    A. 10   B. 40   C. 100   D. 600

15. A centrifugal water pump is direct-driven by a 25 HP 900 RPM electric motor at rated load.
    In order to double the quantity of water delivered, it would be necessary to substitute a motor rated at _____ HP at _____ RPM.

    A. 40; 1200   B. 50; 1200   C. 100; 1800   D. 200; 1800

16. Of the following fire extinguisher ratings, the one which indicates that an extinguisher has the GREATEST capability for extinguishing wood, paper, and electrical fires is

    A. 2-A:16-B:C   B. 4-A:4-B:C
    C. 16-A   D. 8-B

17. Of the following combinations of oil burners and fuel oils, the combination which is the MOST hazardous to fire-up when placing a cold boiler into service is the

   A. compressed air-atomized burner firing light oil
   B. steam-atomized burner firing heavy oil
   C. air-atomized burner firing heavy oil
   D. mechanically-atomized burner firing heavy oil

17.____

18. It is usually desirable to have a program which will create and maintain the interest of workers in safety. Of the following, the one which such a program CANNOT do is to

   A. develop safe work habits
   B. compensate for unsafe procedures
   C. provide a channel of communications between workers and management
   D. give employees a chance to participate in accident prevention activities

18.____

19. Because of a ruptured ammonia tank, the concentration of ammonia gas in a room exceeds 3%.
The wearing of a gas mask, as the only protective device, by a person entering the room is

   A. *recommended,* because the gas mask alone is sufficient protection
   B. *not recommended,* because the ammonia will severely irritate the skin
   C. *not recommended,* because the gas mask is not effective at concentrations above 3%
   D. *not recommended,* because ammonia is flammable

19.____

20. The Occupational Safety and Health Act of 1970 provided for

   A. penalties against employees for safety violations
   B. complete occupational safety against all hazards
   C. standards of employee discipline
   D. employees' right to review a copy of a safety citation against the employer

20.____

21. An aftercooler on a reciprocating air compressor is used PRIMARILY to

   A. increase compressor capacity
   B. improve compressor efficiency
   C. condense the moisture in the compressed air
   D. cool the lubricating oil

21.____

22. The one of the following tasks which is an example of preventive maintenance is

   A. replacing a leaking water pipe nipple
   B. cleaning the cup on a rotary cup burner
   C. cleaning a completely clogged oil strainer
   D. replacing a blown fuse

22.____

23. The four MAIN causes of failure of three-phase electric motors are

   A. dirt, friction, moisture, single-phasing
   B. friction, moisture, single-phasing, vibration
   C. dirt, moisture, single-phasing, vibration
   D. dirt, friction, moisture, vibration

23.____

24. The one of the following electrical control components that may be lubricated is the 24.___

   A. drum controller's copper-to-copper contacts
   B. relay bearing
   C. starter silver contact
   D. shunt spring

25. In the planning of a preventive maintenance program, the FIRST requirement is to 25.___

   A. prepare a maintenance manual
   B. inventory the equipment
   C. inventory the tools available
   D. prepare repair requisitions for all equipment not operating satisfactorily

KEY (CORRECT ANSWERS)

1.	D	11.	D
2.	A	12.	A
3.	C	13.	C
4.	B	14.	A
5.	D	15.	D
6.	B	16.	B
7.	A	17.	D
8.	C	18.	B
9.	B	19.	B
10.	B	20.	D

21.	C
22.	B
23.	D
24.	A
25.	B

EXAMINATION SECTION
TEST 1

DIRECTIONS: Each question or incomplete statement is followed by several suggested answers or completions. Select the one that BEST answers the question or completes the statement. *PRINT THE LETTER OF THE CORRECT ANSWER IN THE SPACE AT THE RIGHT.*

1. In modern ice making, using ammonia equipment, the freezing tank coils should be maintained with the

   A. highest possible pressure consistent with the required brine temperature
   B. lowest possible pressure consistent with the required brine temperature
   C. pressure at a minimum of 10 psig.
   D. pressure at a minimum of 30 psig.

   1.____

2. In ammonia plants, it is IMPORTANT to keep the coils free of oil accumulation by drawing oil out of the coils AT LEAST

   A. weekly B. monthly C. quarterly D. yearly

   2.____

3. A suction line to a compressor that is too SMALL will cause

   A. reduction in the compressor capacity
   B. pressure loss in the line between the suction outlet of the coil and the suction inlet to the compressor
   C. reduction in the overall capacity of the plant
   D. all of the above

   3.____

4. The term *volumetric efficiency* is used in discussing

   A. condenser capacity B. evaporator capacity
   C. compressor capacity D. all of the above

   4.____

5. Non-condensible gases in a refrigerating system

   A. causes a decrease in condensing pressure
   B. is minute and has no way of entering a system under pressure
   C. contributes to high power cost and a reduction in capacity
   D. all of the above

   5.____

6. The capacity of an evaporative condenser depends on

   A. fan volume
   B. the temperature of the entering air
   C. entering air wet bulb
   D. all of the above

   6.____

7. The determining factor in the selection of the method of removing and storing system refrigerant is USUALLY

   A. system size B. nature of refrigerant
   C. system value D. all of the above

   7.____

8. When removing reusable refrigerant from a system, the line to the refrigerant storage drum MUST

   A. contain a sweat fitting
   B. be flexible
   C. be of copper
   D. be of ample size

9. The common methods of determining proper oil charge are

   A. dip stick, paper method, and compressor sight glass
   B. weight measurement, dip stick, liquid line sight glass, and paper method
   C. weight measurement, dip stick, pressure method, and paper method
   D. all of the above

10. When charging or removing oil, the MAIN precautions to be taken are to

    A. use clean oil, watch the crankcase pressure, and slightly overcharge
    B. use clean oil and do not overcharge
    C. watch the crankcase pressure and use dry oil
    D. none of the above

11. The four BASIC methods of determining whether the proper amount of refrigerant is being introduced into the system are

    A. sight glass, weight, pressure, and frost line
    B. bulls eye, weight, pressure, and frost line
    C. sight glass, weight, pressure, and dip stick
    D. all of the above

12. The thermostatic expansion valve has three operating pressures. They are

    A. evaporator, spring, suction
    B. evaporator, bulk, condensing
    C. evaporator, spring, bulb
    D. all of the above

13. The touching surfaces between a thermostatic expansion valve bulb and the suction line MUST be

    A. clean and tight
    B. downstream of the equalizing line
    C. above the coil
    D. all of the above

14. There are three major areas in which care must be taken in designing the multiple refrigeration cycle system. They are

    A. oil return, compressor protection, and electrical overload
    B. oil return, compressor protection, and off-cycle protection
    C. compressor protection, off-cycle protection, and electrical overload
    D. all of the above

15. Pilot operated valves are FREQUENTLY used because 15.____

    A. solenoids are more positive acting
    B. the control point need not be at the valve
    C. they protect against freeze-up
    D. all of the above

16. The oil safety switch is operated by 16.____

    A. oil pressure
    B. the sum of oil pressure and crankcase pressure
    C. the difference between crankcase pressure and oil pressure
    D. all of the above

17. A refrigeration accessory is an article or device that 17.____

    A. adds to the convenience of a system
    B. is not essential in a refrigeration system
    C. adds to the effectiveness of a system
    D. none of the above

18. The material within a strainer drier is known as a 18.____

    A. designate   B. desecrate
    C. desiccant   D. all of the above

19. Before deciding on the capacity of a cooling tower to be installed, it is FIRST necessary 19.____
    to determine the

    A. temperature of the water which will enter the tower
    B. amount of heat that is to be taken up by the condensing water and the amount of water to be circulated
    C. average wind velocity
    D. all of the above

20. The estimated heat gain of a building is 480,000 Btu per hour. 20.____
    What size compressor, in tons, will be required by the air conditioning machine to cool the building?

    A. 100   B. 80   C. 60   D. 40

21. The function of the expansion valve in a refrigerating system is to 21.____

    A. control or meter the liquid flow to the expansion coils or evaporator
    B. regulate the gas flow to the expansion coils or evaporator
    C. control the temperature in the expansion coils or evaporator
    D. all of the above

22. The capacity of a compressor is determined by the 22.____

    A. weight of the refrigerant pumped
    B. temperature and pressure of the evaporator and condenser
    C. volumetric efficiency of the compressor
    D. all of the above

23. Which type of condenser requires the MOST cooling surface? 23.___

    A. Shell and tube B. Submerged
    C. Atmospheric or surface D. All of the above

24. How does the presence of a non-condensable gas in the condenser affect the transmission of heat between the water and refrigerant? 24.___
    The non-condensable gas

    A. displaces the refrigerant
    B. acts as an insulation and reduces the heat transfer
    C. reduces the capacity of the condenser
    D. all of the above

25. Frost on cooling coils affects suction pressure by 25.___

    A. raising the boiling point of the refrigerant
    B. forcing the suction pressure down
    C. raising the suction pressure up
    D. none of the above

26. Human comfort is MOST closely associated with 26.___

    A. temperature and relative humidity of the air
    B. carbon dioxide content of the air
    C. temperature and specific humidity of the air
    D. heat content and dew point of the air

27. An air conditioning cooling coil is actually the _____ of a refrigeration system. 27.___

    A. evaporator B. condenser
    C. expansion valve D. liquid received

28. In a typical commercial refrigeration system such as would be associated with a cold storage warehouse or a walk-in freezer locker, the thermostat in the cooled spaces controls the action of the 28.___

    A. compressor motor starter switch
    B. high pressure cut-out switch
    C. solenoid value in the liquid refrigerant line
    D. all of the above

29. What danger comes from using a low flash point oil in air compressors? 29.___

    A. The oil will not lubricate the cylinder walls
    B. Excessive moisture is formed
    C. Possible explosion in the air compressor, receiver, or piping
    D. All of the above

30. You would know that there is sufficient water going to the cylinder jackets by the temperature of the 30.___

    A. air leaving the compressor
    B. jacket water leaving the compressor
    C. air leaving the intercooler
    D. all of the above

31. What unit of measure is COMMONLY used to indicate the quantity of heat?

    A. Degrees Fahrenheit
    B. Degrees centigrade
    C. B.t.u.
    D. All of the above

32. Humidity is IMPORTANT in cold storage rooms to

    A. prevent shrinkage and drying
    B. lower the temperature
    C. increase formation of frost
    D. all of the above

33. For MAXIMUM capacity and efficiency, the

    A. condenser pressure and the suction pressure should be as near together as possible
    B. suction pressure should be as high as practicable
    C. discharge pressure should be as low as practicable
    D. all of the above

34. A receiver in an air compression system is used to

    A. avoid cooling air before using
    B. reduce the work needed during compression
    C. collect water and grease suspended in the air
    D. increase the air discharge p'ressure

35. The speed of a centrifugal compressor is changed from 1,000 to 3,000 rpm. If the compressor originally delivered 2,000 cfm, the new delivery will be _____ cfm.

    A. 6,000   B. 16,000   C. 22,000   D. 36,000

KEY (CORRECT ANSWERS)

1.	B	16.	C
2.	A	17.	B
3.	D	18.	C
4.	C	19.	B
5.	C	20.	D
6.	D	21.	D
7.	B	22.	C
8.	D	23.	C
9.	A	24.	D
10.	B	25.	D
11.	A	26.	A
12.	C	27.	A
13.	A	28.	C
14.	B	29.	C
15.	B	30.	D

31. C
32. A
33. D
34. C
35. A

MECHANICAL APTITUDE
TOOLS AND THEIR USE

EXAMINATION SECTION
TEST 1

Questions 1-16.

DIRECTIONS: Questions 1 through 16 refer to the tools shown below. The numbers in the answers refer to the numbers beneath the tools.
NOTE: These tools are NOT shown to scale

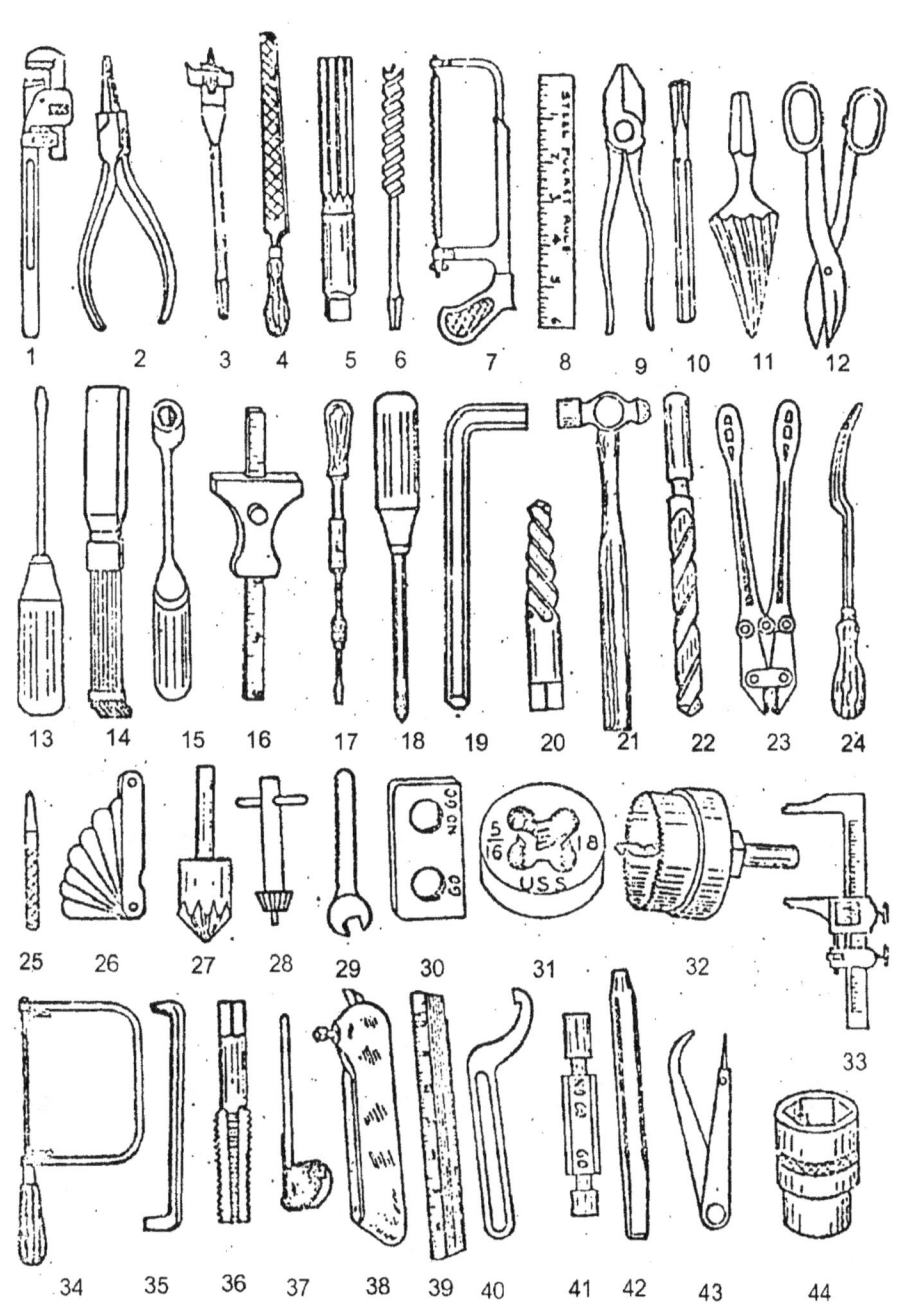

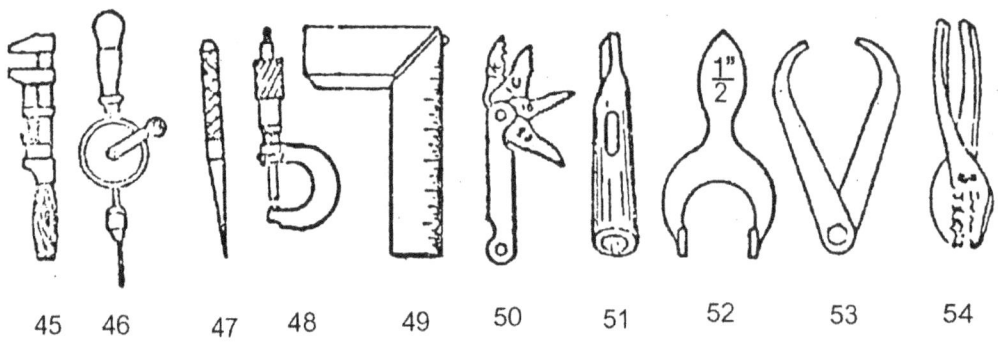

45 46 47 48 49 50 51 52 53 54

1. A 1" x 1" x 1/8" angle iron should be cut by using tool number
   A. 7   B. 12   C. 23   D. 42

2. To peen an iron rivet, you should use tool number
   A. 4   B. 7   C. 21   D. 43

3. The star "drill" is tool number
   A. 5   B. 10   C. 20   D. 22

4. To make holes in sheet metal for sheet metal screws, you should use tool number.
   A. 6   B. 10   C. 36   D. 46

5. To cut through a 3/8" diameter wire rope, you should use tool number
   A. 12   B. 23   C. 42   D. 54

6. To remove cutting burrs from the inside of a steel pipe, you should use tool number
   A. 5   B. 11   C. 14   D. 20

7. The depth of a bored hole may be measured MOST accurately with tool number
   A. 8   B. 16   C. 26   D. 41

8. If the marking on the blade of tool number 7 reads:12"-32", the 32 refers to the
   A. length   B. thickness   C. weight
   D. number of teeth per inch

9. If tool number 6 bears the mark "5", it should be used to drill holes having a diameter of
   A. 5/32"   B. 5/16"   C. 5/8"   D. 5"

10. To determine MOST quickly the number of threads per inch on a bolt, you should use tool number
    A. 8   B. 16   C. 26   D. 50

11. Wood screws, located in positions where the headroom does not permit the use of an ordinary screwdriver, may be removed by using tool number
    A. 17   B. 28   C. 35   D. 46

12. To remove a broken-off piece of 1/2" diameter pipe from a fitting, you should use tool number   12._____

    A. 5   B. 11   C. 20   D. 36

13. The outside diameter of a bushing may be measured MOST accurately with tool number   13._____

    A. 8   B. 26   C. 33   D. 43

14. To re-thread a stud hole in the casting of an elevator motor, you should use tool number   14._____

    A. 5   B. 20   C. 22   D. 36

15. To enlarge slightly a bored hole in a steel plate, you should use tool number   15._____

    A. 5   B. 11   C. 20   D. 36

16. The term "16 oz." should be applied to tool number   16._____

    A. 1   B. 12   C. 21   D. 42

KEYS (CORRECT ANSWERS)

1.	A	9.	B
2.	C	10.	D
3.	B	11.	C
4.	D	12.	C
5.	B	13.	C
6.	B	14.	D
7.	B	15.	A
8.	D	16.	C

TEST 2

Questions 1-11.

DIRECTIONS: Questions 1 through 11 refer to the instruments listed below. Each instrument is listed with an identifying number in front of it.

    1 - Hygrometer   6 - Oscilloscope   11 - 6-foot folding rule
    2 - Ammeter   7 - Frequency meter   12 - Architect's scale
    3 - Voltmeter   8 - Micrometer   13 - Planimeter
    4 - Wattmeter   9 - Vernier calliper   14 - Engineer's scale
    5 - Megger   10 - Wire gage   15 - Ohmmeter

1. The instrument that should be used to *accurately* measure the resistance of a 4,700-ohm resistor is number

    A. 3   B. 4   C. 7   D. 15

2. To measure the current in an electrical circuit, the instrument that should be used is number

    A. 2   B. 7   C. 8   D. 15

3. To measure the insulation resistance of a rubber-covered electrical cable, the instrument that should be used is number

    A. 4   B. 5   C. 8   D. 15

4. An AC motor is hooked up to a power distribution box. In order to check the voltage at the motor terminals, the instrument that should be used is number

    A. 2   B. 3   C. 4   D. 7

5. To measure the shaft diameter of a motor *accurately* to one-thousandth of an inch, the instrument that should be used is number

    A. 8   B. 10   C. 11   D. 14

6. The instrument that should be used to determine whether 25 Hz. or 60 Hz. is present in an electrical circuit is number

    A. 4   B. 5   C. 7   D. 8

7. Of the following, the *proper* instrument to use to determine the diameter of the conductor of a piece of electrical hookup wire is number

    A. 10   B. 11   C. 12   D. 14

8. The amount of electrical power being used in a balanced three-phase circuit should be measured with number

    A. 2   B. 3   C. 4   D. 5

9. The electrical wave form at a given point in an electronic circuit can be observed with number

    A. 2   B. 3   C. 6   D. 7

10. The *proper* instrument to use for measuring the width of a door is number

    A. 11   B. 12   C. 13   D. 14

11. A one-inch hole with a tolerance of plus or minus three-thousandths is reamed in a steel block. The *proper* instrument to accurately check the diameter of the hole is number

    A. 8   B. 9   C. 11   D. 14

12. An oilstone is LEAST likely to be used correctly to sharpen a

    A. scraper   B. chisel   C. knife   D. saw

13. To cut the ends of a number of lengths of wood at an angle of 45 degrees, it would be BEST to use a

    A. mitre-box   B. protractor   C. triangle   D. wooden rule

14. A gouge is a tool used for

    A. planing wood smooth
    B. grinding metal
    C. drilling steel
    D. chiseling wood

15. Holes are usually countersunk when installing

    A. carriage bolts
    B. lag screws
    C. flat-head screws
    D. square nuts

16. A tool that is *generally* used to slightly elongate a round hole in scrap-iron is a

    A. rat-tail file   B. reamer   C. drill   D. rasp

17. When the term "10-24" is used to specify a machine screw, the number 24 refers to the

    A. number of screws per pound
    B. diameter of the screw
    C. length of the screw
    D. number of threads per inch

18. If you were unable to tighten a nut by means of a ratchet wrench because, although the nut turned on with the forward movement of the wrench, it turned off with the backward movement, you should

    A. make the nut hand-tight before using the wrench
    B. reverse the ratchet action
    C. put a few drops of oil on the wrench
    D. use a different socket in the handle

19. If you were installing a long wood screw and found you were unable to drive this screw more than three-quarters of its length by the use of a properly-fitting straight-handled screwdriver, the *proper* SUBSEQUENT action would be for you to

    A. take out the screw and put soap on it
    B. change to the use of a screwdriver-bit and brace
    C. take out the screw and drill a shorter hole before redriving
    D. use a pair of pliers on the blade of the screwdriver

20. Good practice requres that the end of a pipe to be installed in a plumbing system be reamed to remove the inside burr after it has been cut to length. The *purpose* of this reaming is to

    A. restore the original inside diameter of the pipe at the end
    B. remove loose rust
    C. make the threading of the pipe easier
    D. finish the pipe accurately to length

KEYS (CORRECT ANSWERS)

1.	D	11.	B
2.	A	12.	D
3.	B	13.	A
4.	B	14.	D
5.	A	15.	C
6.	C	16.	A
7.	A	17.	D
8.	C	18.	A
9.	C	19.	A
10.	A	20.	A

READING COMPREHENSION
UNDERSTANDING AND INTERPRETING WRITTEN MATERIAL
EXAMINATION SECTION
TEST 1

DIRECTIONS: Each question or incomplete statement is followed by several suggested answers or completions. Select the one that BEST answers the question or completes the statement. *PRINT THE LETTER OF THE CORRECT ANSWER IN THE SPACE AT THE RIGHT.*

Questions 1-2.

DIRECTIONS: Questions 1 and 2 are to be answered SOLELY on the basis of the following paragraph.

When fixing an upper sash cord, you must also remove the lower sash. To do this, the parting strip between the sash must be removed. Now remove the cover from the weight box channel, cut off the cord as before, and pull it over the pulleys. Pull your new cord over the pulleys and down into the channel where it may be fastened to the weight. The cord for an upper sash is cut off 1" or 2" below the pulley with the weight resting on the floor of the pocket and the cord held taut. These measurements allow for slight stretching of the cord. When the cord is cut to length, it can be pulled up over the pulley and tied with a single common knot in the end to fit into the socket in the sash groove. If the knot protrudes beyond the face of the sash, tap it gently to flatten. In this way, it will not become frayed from constant rubbing against the groove.

1. When repairing the upper sash cord, the FIRST thing to do is to
    A. remove the lower sash
    B. cut the existing sash cord
    C. remove the parting strip
    D. measure the length of new cord necessary

1._____

2. According to the above paragraph, the rope may become frayed if the
    A. pulley is too small   B. knot sticks out
    C. cord is too long   D. weight is too heavy

2._____

Questions 3-4.

DIRECTIONS: Questions 3 and 4 are to be answered SOLELY on the basis of the following paragraph.

Repeated burning of the same area should be avoided. Burning should not be done on impervious, shallow, unstable, or highly erodible soils, or on steep slopes—especially in areas subject to heavy rains or rapid snowmelt. When existing vegetation is likely to be killed or seriously weakened by the fire, measures should be taken to assure prompt revegetation of the burned area. Burns should be limited to relatively small proportions of a watershed unit so that the stream channels will be able to carry any increased flows with a minimum of damage.

3. According to the above paragraph, planned burning should be limited to small areas of the watershed because
    A. the fire can be better controlled
    B. existing vegetation will be less likely to be killed
    C. plants will grow quicker in small areas
    D. there will be less likelihood of damaging floods

4. According to the above paragraph, burning USUALLY should be done on soils that
    A. readily absorb moisture
    B. have been burnt before
    C. exist as a thin layer over rock
    D. can be flooded by nearby streams

Questions 5-11.

DIRECTIONS: Questions 5 through 11 are to be answered SOLELY on the basis of the following paragraph.

FUSE INFORMATION

Badly bent or distorted fuse clips cannot be permitted. Sometimes, the distortion or bending is so slight that it escapes notice, yet it may be the cause for fuse failures through the heat that is developed by the poor contact. Occasionally, the proper spring tension of the fuse clips has been destroyed by overheating from loose wire connections to the clips. Proper contact surfaces must be maintained to avoid faulty operation of the fuse. Maintenance men should remove oxides that form on the copper and brass contacts, check the clip pressure, and make sure that contact surfaces are not deformed or bent in any way. When removing oxides, use a well-worn file and remove only the oxide film. Do not use sandpaper or emery cloth as hard particles may come off and become embedded in the contact surfaces. All wire connections to the fuse holders should be carefully inspected to see that they are tight.

5. Fuse failure because of poor clip contact or loose connections is due to the resulting
    A. excessive voltage   B. increased current
    C. lowered resistance   D. heating effect

6. Oxides should be removed from fuse contacts by using
    A. a dull file   B. emery cloth
    C. fine sandpaper   D. a sharp file

7. One result of loose wire connections at the terminal of a fuse clip is stated in the above paragraph to be
    A. loss of tension in the wire
    B. welding of the fuse to the clip
    C. distortion of the clip
    D. loss of tension of the clip

8. Simple reasoning will show that the oxide film referred to is undesirable CHIEFLY because it
   A. looks dull
   B. makes removal of the fuse difficult
   C. weakens the clips
   D. introduces undesirable resistance

9. Fuse clips that are bent very slightly
   A. should be replaced with new clips
   B. should be carefully filed
   C. may result in blowing of the fuse
   D. may prevent the fuse from blowing

10. From the fuse information paragraph, it would be reasonable to conclude that fuse clips
    A. are difficult to maintain
    B. must be given proper maintenance
    C. require more attention than other electrical equipment
    D. are unreliable

11. A safe practical way of checking the tightness of the wire connection to the fuse clips of a live 120-volt lighting circuit is to
    A. feel the connection with your hand to see if it is warm
    B. try tightening with an insulated screwdriver or socket wrench
    C. see if the circuit works
    D. measure the resistance with an ohmmeter

Questions 12-13.

DIRECTIONS: Questions 12 through 13 are to be answered SOLELY on the basis of the following paragraph.

For cast iron pipe lines, the middle ring or sleeve shall have *beveled* ends and shall be high quality cast iron. The middle ring shall have a minimum wall thickness of 3/8" for pipe up to 8", 7/16" for pipe 10" to 30", and 1/2" for pipe over 30", nominal diameter. Minimum length of middle ring shall be 5" for pipe up to 10", 6" for pipe 10" to 30", and 10" for pipe 30" nominal diameter and larger. The middle ring shall not have a center pipe stop, unless otherwise specified.

12. As used in the above paragraph, the word *beveled* means MOST NEARLY
    A. straight   B. slanted   C. curved   D. rounded

13. In accordance with the above paragraph, the middle ring of a 24" nominal diameter pipe would have a minimum wall thickness and length of _____ thick and _____ long.
    A. 3/8"; 5:
    B. 3/8"; 6"
    C. 7/16"; 6"
    D. 1/2"; 6"

Questions 14-17.

DIRECTIONS: Questions 14 through 17 are to be answered SOLELY on the basis of the following paragraph.

Operators spotting loads with long booms and working around men need the smooth, easy operation and positive control of uniform pressure swing clutches. There are no jerks or grabs with these large disc-type clutches because there is always even pressure over the entire clutch lining surface. In the conventional band-type swing clutch, the pressure varies between dead and live ends of the band. The uniform pressure swing clutch has excellent provision for heat dissipation. The driving elements, which are always rotating, have a great number of fins cast in them. This gives them an impeller or blower action for cooling, resulting in longer life and freedom from frequent adjustment.

14. According to the above paragraph, it may be said that conventional band-type swing clutches have
    A. even pressure on the clutch lining
    B. larger contact area
    C. smaller contact area
    D. uneven pressure on the clutch lining

14.____

15. According to the above paragraph, machines equipped with uniform pressure swing clutches will
    A. give better service under all conditions
    B. require no clutch adjustment
    C. give positive control of hoist
    D. provide better control of swing

15.____

16. According to the above paragraph, it may be said that the rotation of the driving elements of the uniform pressure swing clutch is ALWAYS
    A. continuous   B. constant
    C. varying   D. uncertain

16.____

17. According to the above paragraph, freedom from frequent adjustment is due to the
    A. operator's smooth, easy operation
    B. positive control of the clutch
    C. cooling effect of the rotating fins
    D. larger contact area of the bigger clutch

17.____

Questions 18-22.

DIRECTIONS: Questions 18 through 22 are to be answered SOLELY on the basis of the following paragraphs.

Exhaust valve clearance adjustment on diesel engines is very important for proper operation of the engine. Insufficient clearance between the exhaust valve stem and the rocker arm causes a loss of compression and, after a while, burning of the valves and valve seat inserts. On the other hand, too much valve clearance will result in noisy operation of the engine.

Exhaust valves that are maintained in good operating condition will result in efficient combustion in the engine. Valve seats must be true and unpitted, and valve stems must work smoothly within the valve guides. Long valve life will result from proper maintenance and operation of the engine.

Engine operating temperatures should be maintained between 160°F and 185°F. Low operating temperatures result in incomplete combustion and the deposit of fuel lacquers on valves.

18. According to the above paragraphs, too much valve clearance will cause the engine to operate
    A. slowly   B. noisily   C. smoothly   D. cold

    18._____

19. On the basis of the information given in the above paragraphs, operating temperatures of a diesel engine should be between
    A. 125°F and 130°F   B. 140°F and 150°F
    C. 160°F and 185°F   D. 190°F and 205°F

    19._____

20. According to the above paragraphs, the deposit of fuel lacquers on valves is caused by
    A. high operating temperatures
    B. insufficient valve clearance
    C. low operating temperatures
    D. efficient combustion

    20._____

21. According to the above paragraphs, for efficient operation of the engine, valve seats must
    A. have sufficient clearance
    B. be true and unpitted
    C. operate at low temperatures
    D. be adjusted regularly

    21._____

22. According to the above paragraphs, a loss of compression is due to insufficient clearance between the exhaust valve stem and the
    A. rocker arm   B. valve seat
    C. valve seat inserts D. valve guides

    22._____

Questions 23-25.

DIRECTIONS: Questions 23 through 25 are to be answered SOLELY on the basis of the following excerpt:

A SPECIFICATION FOR ELECTRIC WORK FOR THE CITY

Breakers shall be equipped with magnetic blowout coils...Handles of breakers shall be trip-free...Breakers shall be designed to carry 100% of trip rating continuously; to have inverse time delay tripping above 100% of trip rating...

23. According to the above paragraph, the breaker shall have provision for
    A. resetting   B. arc quenching
    C. adjusting trip time D. adjusting trip rating

    23._____

24. According to the above paragraph, the breaker
    A. shall trip easily at exactly 100% of trip rating
    B. shall trip instantly at a little more than 100% of trip rating
    C. should be constructed so that it shall not be possible to prevent it from opening on overload or short circuit by holding the handle in the ON position
    D. shall not trip prematurely at 100% of trip rating

    24._____

25. According to the above paragraph, the breaker shall trip
    A. instantaneously as soon as 100% of trip rating is reached
    B. instantaneously as soon as 100% of trip rating is exceeded
    C. more quickly the greater the current, once 100% of trip rating is exceeded
    D. after a predetermined fixed time lapse, once 100% of trip rating is reached

KEY (CORRECT ANSWERS)

1.	C		11.	B
2.	B		12.	B
3.	D		13.	C
4.	A		14.	D
5.	D		15.	D
6.	A		16.	A
7.	D		17.	C
8.	D		18.	B
9.	C		19.	C
10.	B		20.	C

21. B
22. A
23. B
24. C
25. C

TEST 2

DIRECTIONS: Each question or incomplete statement is followed by several suggested answers or completions. Select the one that BEST answers the question or completes the statement. *PRINT THE LETTER OF THE CORRECT ANSWER IN THE SPACE AT THE RIGHT.*

Questions 1-4.

DIRECTIONS: Questions 1 through 4 are to be answered SOLELY on the basis of the following paragraph.

A low pressure hot water boiler shall include a relief valve or valves of a capacity such that with the heat generating equipment operating at maximum, the pressure cannot rise more than 20 percent above the maximum allowable working pressure (set pressure) if that is 30 p.s.i. gage or less, nor more than 10 percent if it is more than 30 p.s.i. gage. The difference between the set pressure and the pressure at which the valve is relieving is known as *over-pressure or accumulation.* If the steam relieving capacity in pounds per hour is calculated, it shall be determined by dividing by 1,000 the maximum BTU output at the boiler nozzle obtainable from the heat generating equipment, or by multiplying the square feet of heating surface by five.

1. In accordance with the above paragraph, the capacity of a relief valve should be computed on the basis of
    A. size of boiler
    B. maximum rated capacity of generating equipment
    C. average output of the generating equipment
    D. minimum capacity of generating equipment

1._____

2. In accordance with the above paragraph, with a set pressure of 30 p.s.i. gage, the overpressure should not be more than _____ p.s.i.
    A. 3   B. 6   C. 33   D. 36

2._____

3. In accordance with the above paragraph, a relief valve should start relieving at a pressure equal to the
    A. set pressure
    B. over pressure
    C. over pressure minus set pressure
    D. set pressure plus over pressure

3._____

4. In accordance with the above paragraph, the steam relieving capacity can be computed by
    A. *multiplying* the maximum BTU output by 5
    B. *dividing* the pounds of steam per hour by 1,000
    C. *dividing* the maximum BTU output by the square feet of heating surface
    D. *dividing* the maximum BTU output by 1,000

4._____

Questions 5-8.

DIRECTIONS: Questions 5 through 8 are to be answered SOLELY on the basis of the following paragraph.

Air conditioning units requiring a minimum rate of flow of water in excess of one-half (1/2) gallon per minute shall be metered. Air conditioning equipment with a refrigeration unit which has a definite rate of capacity in tons or fractions thereof, the charge will be at the rate of $30 per annum per ton capacity from the date installed to the date when the supply is metered. Such units, when equipped with an approved water-conserving device, shall be charged at the rate of $4.50 per annum per ton capacity from the date installed to the date when the supply is metered.

5. A man who was in the market for air conditioning equipment was considering three different units. Unit 1 required a flow of 28 gallons of water per hour; Unit 2 required 30 gallons of water per hour; Unit 3 required 32 gallons of water per hour. The man asked the salesman which units would require the installation of a water meter. According to the above passage, the salesman SHOULD answer:
    A. All three units require meters
    B. Units 2 and 3 require meters
    C. Unit 3 only requires a meter
    D. None of the units require a meter

6. Suppose that air conditioning equipment with a refrigeration unit of 10 tons was put in operation on October 1; and in the following year on July 1, a meter was installed. According to the above passage, the charge for this period would be _____ the annual rate.
    A. twice   B. equal to
    C. three-fourths   D. one-fourth

7. The charge for air conditioning equipment which has no refrigeration unit
    A. is $30 per year
    B. is $25.50 per year
    C. is $4.50 per year
    D. cannot be determined from the above passage

8. The charge for air conditioning equipment with a seven-ton refrigeration unit equipped with an approved water-conserving device
    A. is $4.50 per year
    B. is $25.50 per year
    C. is $31.50 per year
    D. cannot be determined from the above passage

Questions 9-14.

DIRECTIONS: Questions 9 through 14 are to be answered SOLELY on the basis of the following paragraph.

The city makes unremitting efforts to keep the water free from pollution. An inspectional force under a sanitary expert is engaged in patrolling the watersheds to see that the department's sanitary regulations are observed. Samples taken daily from various points in the water supply system are examined and analyzed at the three laboratories maintained by the department. All water before delivery to the distribution mains is treated with chlorine to destroy bacteria. In addition, some water is aerated to free it from gases and, in some cases, from microscopic organisms. Generally, microscopic organisms which develop in the reservoirs and at times impart an unpleasant taste and odor to the water, though in no sense harmful to health, are destroyed by treatment with copper sulfate and by chlorine dosage. None of the supplies is filtered, but the quality of the water supplied by the city is excellent for all purposes, and it is clear and wholesome.

9. According to the above paragraph, microscopic organisms are removed from the water supplied to the city by means of
    A. chlorine alone
    B. chlorine, aeration, and filtration
    C. chlorine, aeration, filtration, and sampling
    D. copper sulfate, chlorine, and aeration

9._____

10. Microscopic organisms in the water supply GENERALLY are
    A. a health menace
    B. impossible to detect
    C. not harmful to health
    D. not destroyed in the water

10._____

11. The MAIN function of the inspectional force, as described in the above paragraph, is to
    A. take samples of water for analysis
    B. enforce sanitary regulations
    C. add chlorine to the water supply
    D. inspect water-use meters

11._____

12. According to the above paragraph, chlorine is added to water before entering the
    A. watersheds
    B. reservoirs
    C. distribution mains
    D. run-off areas

12._____

13. Of the following suggested headings or titles for the above paragraph, the one that BEST tells what the paragraph is about is
    A. QUALITY OF WATER
    B. CHLORINATION OF WATER
    C. TESTING OF WATER
    D. BACTERIA IN WATER

13._____

14. The MOST likely reason for taking samples of water for examination and analysis from various points in the water supply system is:
    A. The testing points are convenient to the department's laboratories
    B. Water from one part of the system may be made undrinkable by a local condition
    C. The samples can be distributed equally among the three laboratories
    D. The hardness or softness of water varies from place to place

14._____

Questions 15-17.

DIRECTIONS: Questions 15 through 17 are to be answered SOLELY on the basis of the following paragraph.

A building measuring 200' x 100' at the street is set back 20' on all sides at the 15th floor, and an additional 10' on all sides at the 30th floor. The building is 35 stories high.

15. The floor area of the 16th floor is MOST NEARLY _____ sq. ft.   15._____
    A. 20,000   B. 14,400   C. 9,600   D. 7,500

16. The floor area of the 35th floor is MOST NEARLY _____ sq. ft.   16._____
    A. 20,000   B. 13,900   C. 7,500   D. 5,600

17. The floor area of the 16th floor, compared to the floor area of the 2nd floor, is   17._____
    MOST NEARLY _____ as much.
    A. three-fourths (3/4)   B. two-thirds (2/3)
    C. one-half (1/2)   D. four-tenths (4/10)

Question 18.

DIRECTIONS: Question 18 is to be answered SOLELY on the basis of the following paragraph.

Experience has shown that, in general, a result of the installation of meters on services not previously metered is to reduce the amount of water consumed, but is not necessarily to reduce the peak load on plumbing systems. The permissible head loss through meters at their rated maximum flow is 20 p.s.i. The installation of a meter may therefore appreciably lower the pressures available in fixtures on a plumbing system.

18. According to the above paragraph, a water meter may   18._____
    A. limit the flow in the plumbing system of 20 p.s.i.
    B. reduce the peak load on the plumbing system
    C. increase the overall amount of water consumed
    D. reduce the pressure in the plumbing system

Question 19.

DIRECTIONS: Question 19 is to be answered SOLELY on the basis of the following paragraph.

Spring comes without trumpets to a city. The asphalt is a wilderness that does not quicken overnight; winds blow gritty with cinders instead of merry with the smells of earth and fertilizer. Women wear their gardens on their hats. But spring is a season in the city, and it has its own harbingers, constant as daffodils. Shop windows change their colors, people walk more slowly on the streets, what one can see of the sky has a bluer tone. Pulitzer prizes awake and sing and matinee tickets go-a-begging. But gayer than any of these are the carousels, which are already in sheltered places, beginning to turn with the sound of springtime itself. They are the earliest and the truest and the oldest of all the urban signs.

19. In the passage above, the word *harbingers* means   19._____
    A. storms   B. truths   C. virtues   D. forerunners

Questions 20-22.

DIRECTIONS: Questions 20 through 22 are to be answered SOLELY on the basis of the following paragraph.

Gas heaters include manually operated, automatic, and instantaneous heaters. Some heaters are equipped with a thermostat which controls the fuel supply so that when the water falls below a predetermined temperature, the fuel is automatically turned on. In some types, the hot-water storage tank is well-insulated to economize the use of fuel. Instantaneous heaters are arranged so that the opening of a faucet on the hot-water pipe will increase the flow of fuel, which is ignited by a continuously burning pilot light to heat the water to from 120° to 130°F. The possibility that the pilot light will die out offers a source of danger in the use of automatic appliances which depend on a pilot light. Gas and oil heaters are dangerous, and they should be designed to prevent the accumulation, in a confined space within the heater, of a large volume of an explosive mixture.

20. According to the above passage, the opening of a hot-water faucet on a hot-water pipe connected to an instantaneous hot-water heater will the pilot light.
    A. *increase* the temperature of
    B. *increase* the flow of fuel to
    C. *decrease* the flow of fuel to
    D. *have a marked effect* on

21. According to the above passage, the fuel is automatically turned on in a heater equipped with a thermostat whenever
    A. the water temperature drops below 120°F
    B. the pilot light is lit
    C. the water temperature drops below some predetermined temperature
    D. a hot water supply is opened

22. According to the above passage, some hot-water storage tanks are well-insulated to
    A. accelerate the burning of the fuel
    B. maintain the water temperature between 120° and 130°F
    C. prevent the pilot light from being extinguished
    D. minimize the expenditure of fuel

Question 23.

DIRECTIONS: Question 23 is to be answered SOLELY on the basis of the following paragraph.

Breakage of the piston under high-speed operation has been the commonest fault of disc piston meters. Various techniques are adopted to prevent this, such as *throttling* the meter, cutting away the edge of the piston, or reinforcing it, but these are simply makeshifts.

23. As used in the above paragraph, the word *throttling* means MOST NEARLY
    A. enlarging   B. choking
    C. harnessing   D. dismantling

Questions 24-25.

DIRECTIONS: Questions 24 and 25 are to be answered SOLELY on the basis of the following paragraph.

One of the most common and objectionable difficulties occurring in a drainage system is trap seal loss. This failure can be attributed directly to inadequate ventilation of the trap and the subsequent negative and positive pressures which occur. A trap seal may be lost either by siphonage and/or back pressure. Loss of the trap seal by siphonage is the result of a negative pressure in the drainage system. The seal content of the trap is forced by siphonage into the waste piping of the drainage system through exertion of atmospheric pressure on the fixture side of the trap seal.

24. According to the above paragraph, a positive pressure is a direct result of
    A. siphonage
    B. unbalanced trap seal
    C. poor ventilation
    D. atmospheric pressure

25. According to the above paragraph, the water in the trap is forced into the drain pipe by
    A. atmospheric pressure
    B. back pressure
    C. negative pressure
    D. back pressure on fixture side of seal

KEY (CORRECT ANSWERS)

1.	B	11.	B
2.	B	12.	C
3.	D	13.	A
4.	D	14.	B
5.	C	15.	C
6.	C	16.	D
7.	D	17.	C
8.	C	18.	D
9.	D	19.	B
10.	C	20.	B

21. C
22. D
23. B
24. C
25. A

HEATING AND ENVIRONMENTAL CONTROL

CONTENTS

		Page
I.	Introduction	1
II.	Definitions	1
III.	Fuels	3
IV.	Central Heating Units	6
V.	Fuel-Burning Procedures and Automatic Firing Equipment	9
VI.	Refractory	11
VII.	Heating Systems	11
VIII.	Domestic Hot Water Jack Stoves (Coal Stoves)	23
IX.	Hazardous Installations	23

HEATING AND ENVIRONMENTAL CONTROL

I. Introduction

The function of a heating system is to provide for human comfort. The variables to be controlled are temperature, air motion, and relative humidity. Temperature must be maintained uniformly throughout the heated area. Field experience indicates a variation from 6 to 10 degrees F from floor to ceiling. The adequacy of the heating device and the tightness of the structure or room determine the degree of personal comfort within the dwelling.

Coal, wood, oil, gas, and electricity are the main sources of heat energy. Heating systems commonly used are steam, hot water, and hot air. The housing inspector should have a knowledge of the various heating fuels and systems to be able to determine their adequacy and safety in operation. To cover fully all aspects of the heating system, the entire area and physical components of the system must be considered.

II. Definitions

A **Anti-flooding Control** — A safety control that shuts off fuel and ignition when excessive fuel accumulates in the appliance.

B **Appliance:**
1. **High-heat** — a unit that operates with flue entrance temperature of combustion products above 1,500°F.
2. **Medium heat** — same as high-heat, except above 600°F.
3. **Low heat** — same as high heat, except below 600°F.

C **Boiler:**
1. **High pressure** – a boiler furnishing pressure at 15 psi or more.
2. **Low pressure** — (hot water or steam) — a boiler furnishing steam at a pressure less than 15 psi or hot water not more than 30 psi.

D **Burner** — A device that provides the mixing of fuel, air, and ignition in a combustion chamber.

E **Chimney** — A vertical shaft containing one or more passageways.
1. **Factory-built chimney** — a tested and accredited flue for venting gas appliances, incinerators and solid or liquid fuel-burning appliances.
2. **Masonry chimney** — a field-constructed chimney built of masonry and lined with terra cotta flue or firebrick.
3. **Metal chimney** — a field-constructed chimney of metal.
4. **Chimney Connector** — A pipe or breeching that connects the heating appliance to the chimney.

F **Clearance** — The distance separating the appliance, chimney connector, plenum, and flue from the nearest surface of combustible material.

G **Central Heating System** — A boiler or furnace, flue connected, installed as an integral part of the structure and designed to supply heat adequately for the structure.

H **Controls:**
1. **High-low limit control** — an automatic control that responds to liquid level changes and pressure or temperature changes and that limits operation of the appliance to be controlled.

2 **Primary safety control** — the automatic safety control intended to prevent abnormal discharge of fuel at the burner in case of ignition failure or flame failure.

3 **Combustion safety control** — a primary safety control that responds to flame properties, sensing the presence of flame and causing fuel to be shut off in event of flame failure.

I **Convector** — A convector is a radiator that supplies a maximum amount of heat by convection, using many closely-spaced metal fins fitted onto pipes that carry hot water or steam and thereby heat the circulating air.

J **Conversion** — a boiler or furnace, flue connected, originally designed for solid fuel but converted for liquid or gas fuel.

K **Damper** — a valve for regulating draft. Generally located on the exhaust side of the combustion chamber, usually in the chimney connector.

L **Draft Hood** — a device placed in and made a part of the vent connector (chimney connector or smoke pipe) from an appliance, or in the appliance itself, that is designed to (a) ensure the ready escape of the products of combustion in the event of no draft, back-draft, or stoppage beyond the draft hood; (b) prevent backdraft from entering the appliance; (c) neutralize the effect of stack action of the chimney flue upon appliance operation.

M **Draft Regulator** — a device that functions to maintain a desired draft in oil-fired appliances by automatically reducing the chimney draft to the desired value. Sometimes this device is referred to, in the field, as air-balance, air-stat, or flue velocity control.

N **Fuel Oil** — a liquid mixture or compound derived from petroleum that does not emit flammable vapor below a temperature of 125°F.

O **Heat** — the warming of a building, apartment, or room by a stove, furnace, or electricity.

P **Heating Plant** — the furnace, boiler, or the other heating devices used to generate steam, hot water, or hot air, which then is circulated through a distribution system. It uses coal, gas, oil, or wood as its source of heat.

Q **Limit Control** — a thermostatic device installed in the duct system to shut off the supply of heat at a predetermined temperature of the circulated air.

R **Oil Burner** — a device for burning oil in heating appliances such as boilers, furnaces, water heaters, and ranges. A burner of this type may be a pressure-atomizing gun type, a horizontal or vertical rotary type, or a mechanical or natural draft-vaporizing type.

S **Oil Stove** — a flue-connected, self-contained, self-supporting oil-burning range or room heater equipped with an integral tank not exceeding 10 gallons; it may be designed to be connected to a separate oil supply tank.

T **Plenum Chamber** — an air compartment to which one or more distributing air ducts are connected.

U **Pump, Automatic Oil** — a device that automatically pumps oil from the supply tank and delivers it in specific quantities to an oil-burning appliance. The pump or device is designed to stop pumping automatically in case of a breakage of the oil supply line.

V **Radiant Heat** — a method of heating a building by means of electric coils, hot water, or steam pipes installed in the floors, walls, or ceilings.

W **Register** — a grille-covered opening in a floor or wall through which hot or cold air can be introduced into a room. It may or may not be arranged to permit closing of the grille.

X **Room Heater** — a self-contained, free-standing heating appliance intended for installation in the space being heated and not intended for duct connection (space heater).

Y **Smoke Detector** — a device installed in the plenum chamber or in the main supply air duct of an air-conditioning system to shut off the blower automatically and close a fire damper in the presence of smoke.

Z **Tank** — a separate tank connected, directly or by pump, to an oil-burning appliance.

AA **Thimble** — a term applied to a metal or terra cotta lining for a chimney or furnace pipe.

BB **Valve — Main Shut-off Valve** — a manually operated valve in an oil line for the purpose of turning on or off the oil supply to the burner.

CC **Vent System** — the gas vent or chimney and vent connector, if used, assembled to form a continuous, unobstructed passageway from the gas appliance to the outside atmosphere for the purpose of removing vent gases.

III. Fuels

A Coal

Classification and composition — the four types of coal are: anthracite, bituminous, sub-bituminous, and lignitic.

Coal is prepared in many sizes and combinations of sizes. The combustible portions of the coal are fixed carbons, volatile matter (hydrocarbons), and small amounts of sulfur. In combination with these are non-combustible elements composed of moisture and impurities that form ash. The various types differ in heat content. The heat content is determined by analysis and is expressed in British Thermal Units (BTU) per pound. The type and size of coal used are determined by the availability and by the equipment in which it is burned.

The type and size of coal must be proper for the particular heating unit; that is, the furnace grate and flue size must be designed for the particular type of coal. Excessive coal gas can be generated through improper firing as a result of improper fuel or improper furnace design, or both.

The owner should be questioned about his procedure for adding coal to his furnace. It should be explained that a period of time must be allowed to pass before damping to prevent the release of excessive coal gas. This should also be done before damping for the night or other periods when full draft is not required.

Improper coal furnace operation can result in an extremely hazardous and unhealthful occupancy — the inspector should be able to offer helpful operational procedures. Ventilation of the area surrounding the furnace is very important in order to prevent heat buildup and to supply air for combustion.

B Fuel Oil

Fuel oils are derived from petroleum, which consists primarily of compounds of hydrogen and carbon (hydrocarbons) and smaller amounts of nitrogen and sulfur.

Classification of fuel oils Domestic fuel oils are controlled by rigid specifications. Six grades of fuel oil are generally used in healing systems; the lighter two grades are used primarily for domestic heating.

These grades are:

1 **Grade Number 1** — A volatile, distillate oil for use in burners that prepare fuel for burning solely by vaporization (oil-fired space heaters).

2 **Grade Number 2** — A moderate-weight, volatile, distillate oil used for burners that prepare oil for burning by a combination of vaporization and atomization. This grade of oil is commonly used in domestic heating furnaces.

3 **Grade Number 3** — A low-viscosity, distillate oil used in burners wherein fuel and air are prepared for burning solely by atomization.

4 **Grade Number 4** — A medium-viscosity oil used in burners without preheating. (Small industrial or apartment house applications.)

5 **Grade Number 5** — A medium-viscosity oil used in burners with preheaters that require an oil of lower viscosity than Grade Number 6. (Industrial or apartment house application.)

6 **Grade Number 6** — A high-viscosity oil for use in burners with preheating facilities adequate for handling oil of high viscosity. (Industrial applications.)

7 **Heat content** — Heating values of oil vary from approximately 152,000 BTU per gallon for Number 6 oil to 136,000 BTU per gallon for Number 1.

Oil is more widely used today than coal and provides a more automatic source of heat and comfort. It also requires more complicated systems and controls.

If the oil supply is used within the basement or cellar area, certain basic regulations must be followed (see Figure 1). No more than two 275-gallon tanks may be installed above ground in the lowest story of any one building. The tank shall not be closer than 7 feet horizontally to any boiler, furnace, stove, or exposed flame. Fuel oil lines should be embedded in a concrete or cement floor or protected against damage if they run across the floor. Bach tank must have a shutoff valve that will stop the flow from each tank if a leak develops in the line to or in the burner itself.

The tank or tanks must be vented to the outside, and a gauge showing the quantity of oil in the tank or tanks must be tight and operative. Tanks must be off the floor and on a stable base to prevent settlement or movement that may rupture the connections.

A buried outside tank installation is shown in Figure 2.

C Gas

Commercial gas fuels are colorless gases. Some have a characteristic pungent odor, while others are odorless and cannot be detected by smell. Although gas fuels are easily handled in heating equipment, their presence in air in appreciable quantities becomes a serious health hazard. Gases diffuse readily in the air, making explosive mixtures possible. (A proportion of combustible gas and air that is ignited burns with such a high velocity that an explosive force is created.) Because of these characteristics of gas fuels, precautions must be taken to prevent leaks, and care must be exercised when gas-fired equipment is lit.

Classification of gas - Gas is broadly classified as natural or manufactured.

1. **Manufactured Gas** — This gas as distributed is usually a combination of certain proportions of gases produced by two or more processes as obtained from coke, coal, and petroleum. Its BTU value per cubic foot is generally closely regulated, and costs are determined on a guaran-

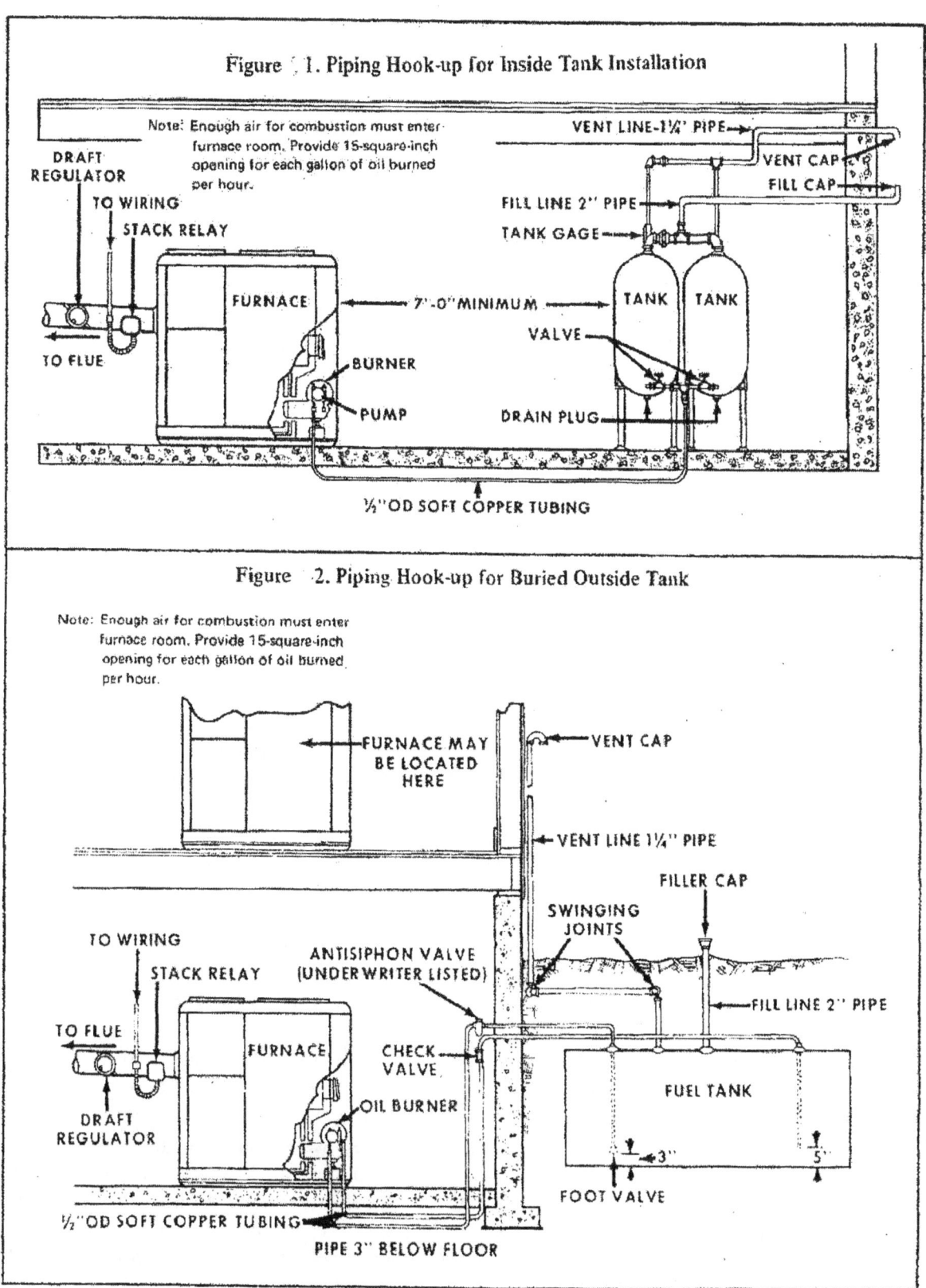

Figure 1. Piping Hook-up for Inside Tank Installation

Figure 2. Piping Hook-up for Buried Outside Tank

teed BTU basis, usually 520 to 540 per cubic foot.

2. **Natural Gas** — This gas is a mixture of several combustible and inert gases. It is one of the richest gases and is obtained from wells ordinarily located in petroleum-producing areas. The heat content may vary from 700 to 1,300 BTU's per cubic foot with a generally accepted average figure of 1,000 BTU's per cubic foot. Natural gases are distributed through pipe lines to point of utilization and are often mixed with manufactured gas to maintain a guaranteed BTU content.

3. **Liquified Petroleum Gas** — Principal products of liquified petroleum gas are butane and propane. Butane and propane are derived from natural gas or petroleum refinery gas and are chemically classified as hydrocarbon gases.

Specifically, butane and propane are on the borderline between a liquid and a gaseous state. At ordinary atmospheric pressure butane is a gas above 33°F and propane a gas at -42°F. These gases are mixed to produce commercial gas suitable for various climatic conditions. Butane and propane are heavier than air. The heat content of butane is 3,274 BTU's per cubic foot while that of propane is 2,519.

The gas burner should be equipped with an automatic cutoff in case the flame fails. Shutoff valves should be located within 1 foot of the burner connection and on the output side of the meter.

CAUTION — Liquified petroleum gas is heavier than air; therefore, the gas will accumulate at the bottom of confined areas. If a leak should develop, care should be taken to ventilate the appliance before lighting.

D Electricity

Electricity is gaining popularity in many regions, particularly where costs are competitive with other sources of heat energy. With an electric system, the housing inspector should rely mainly on the electrical inspector for proper installation. There are a few items, however, to be concerned with to ensure safe use of the equipment. Check to see that the units are accredited testing agency approved and installed according to the manufacturer's specifications. Most convector-type units are required to be installed at least 2 inches above the floor level, not only to ensure that proper convection currents are established through the unit, but also to allow sufficient air insulation from any combustible flooring material. The housing inspector should check for curtains that extend too close to the unit or loose, long pile rugs that are too close. A distance of 6 inches on the floor and 12 inches on the walls should separate rug or curtains from the appliance.

Radiant heating plastered into the ceiling or wall is technical in nature and not a part of the housing inspector's competence. He should, however, be knowledgeable about the system used. These systems are relatively new. If wires are bared in the plastering they should be treated as open and exposed wiring.

IV. Central Heating Units

The boiler should be placed in a separate room whenever possible; in new construction this is usually required. In most housing inspections, however, we are dealing with existing conditions; therefore, we must adapt the situation as closely as possible to acceptable safety standards. In many old buildings the furnace is located in the center of the cellar or basement, and this location does not lend itself for practical conversion to a boiler room.

A Boiler Location

Consider the physical requirements for a boiler room.

1. Ventilation — More circulating air is required for the boiler room than for a habitable room, in order to reduce the heat buildup caused by the boiler or furnace as well as to supply oxygen for combustion.

2. Fire Protection Rating — As specified by various codes (fire code, building code, and insurance underwriters) the fire regulations must be strictly adhered to in areas surrounding the boiler or furnace. This minimum dimension from which a boiler or furnace is to be spaced from a wall or ceiling is shown in Figure 3.

Many times the enclosure of the furnace or boiler creates a problem of providing adequate air supply and ventilation for the room. Where codes and local authority permit, it may be more practical to place the furnace or boiler in an open area. The ceiling above the furnace should be fire protected to a distance of 3 feet beyond all furnace or boiler appurtenances and this area should be free of all storage material. The furnace or boiler should be set on a firm foundation of concrete if located in the cellar or basement. If the codes permit furnace installations on the first floor, then the building code must be consulted for proper setting and location.

B Heating Boilers

Boilers may be classified according to several kinds of characteristics. The material may be cast iron or steel. Their construction may be section, portable, fire-tube, water-tube, or special. Domestic heating boilers are generally of low-pressure type with a maximum working pressure of 15 pounds per square inch for steam and 30 pounds per square inch for hot water.

All boilers have a combustion chamber for burning fuel. Automatic fuel-firing devices help supply the fuel and control the combustion. Handfiring is accomplished by the provision of a grate, ash pit, and controllable drafts to admit air under the fuel bed and over it through slots in the firing door. A check draft is required at the smoke pipe connection to control chimney draft. The gas passes from the combustion chamber to the flue, passages (smoke pipe) designed for maximum possible transfer of heat from the gas. Provisions must be made for cleaning flue passages.

The term boiler is applied to the single heat source that can supply either steam or hot-water (boiler is often called a heater).

Cast iron boilers are generally classified as:
1. Square or rectangular boilers with vertical sections.
2. Round, square, or rectangular boilers with horizontal pancake sections.

Cast iron boilers are usually shipped in sections and assembled at the site.

C Steel Boilers

Most steel boilers are assembled units with welded steel construction and are called portable boilers. Larger boilers are installed in refractory brick settings built on the site. Above the combustion chamber a group of tubes is suspended, usually horizontally, between two headers. If flue gases pass through the tubes and water surrounds them, the boiler is designated as the fire-tube type. When water flows through the tubes, it is termed water-tube. Fire-tube is the predominant type.

D Heating Furnaces

Heating furnaces are the heat sources used when air is the heat-carrying medium. When air circulates because of the different densities of the heated and cooled air, the furnace is a gravity type. A fan may be included for the air circulation; this type is called a mechanical warm-air furnace. Furnaces may be of cast iron or steel and burn various types of fuel.

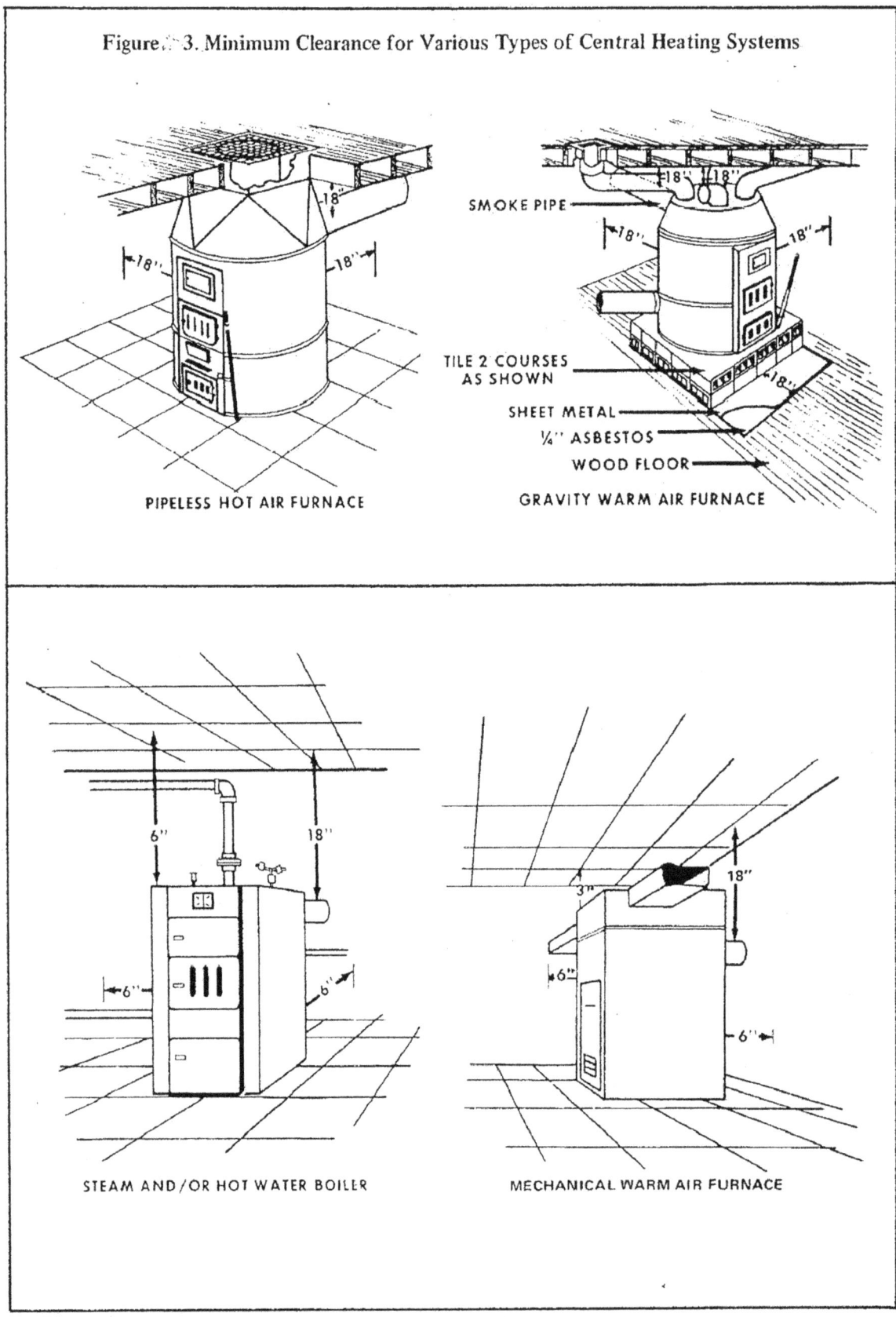

Figure 3. Minimum Clearance for Various Types of Central Heating Systems

V. Fuel-Burning Procedures and Automatic Firing Equipment

A Coal — Many localities throughout the nation still use coal as a heating fuel.

1. **Hand Stoking** - In many older furnaces, the coal is stoked or fed into the fire box by hand.

2. **Automatic Stokers** - The single-retort, underfeed-type bituminous coal stoker is the most commonly used domestic-type steam or hot water boiler (see Figure 4). The stoker consists of a coal hopper, a screw for conveying coal from hopper to retort, a fan that supplies air for combustion, a transmission for driving coalfeed and fan, and an electric motor for supplying power. The air for combustion is admitted to the fuel through tuyeres at the top of the retort. The stoker feeds coal to the furnace intermittently in accordance with the temperature or pressure demands.

B Oil Burners — Oil burners are broadly designated as distillate, domestic, and commercial or industrial. Distillate burners are usually found in oil-fired space heaters. Domestic oil burners are usually power driven and are used in domestic heating plants. Commercial or industrial burners are used in larger central-heating plants for steam or power generation.

1. **Domestic Oil Burners** — These vaporize and atomize the oil, and deliver a predetermined quantity of oil and air to the combustion chambers. Domestic oil burners operate automatically to maintain a desired temperature.

    a. **Gun-type burners** — These burners atomize the oil either by oil pressure or by low-pressure air forced through a nozzle.

The oil system pressure atomizing burner (see Figure 5) consists of a strainer, pump, pressure-regulating valve, shutoff valve, and atomizing nozzle. The air system consists of a power-drive fan and an air tube that surrounds the nozzle and electrode assembly. The fan and oil pump are generally connected directly to the motor. Oil pressures normally used are about 100 pounds per square inch, but pressures con-

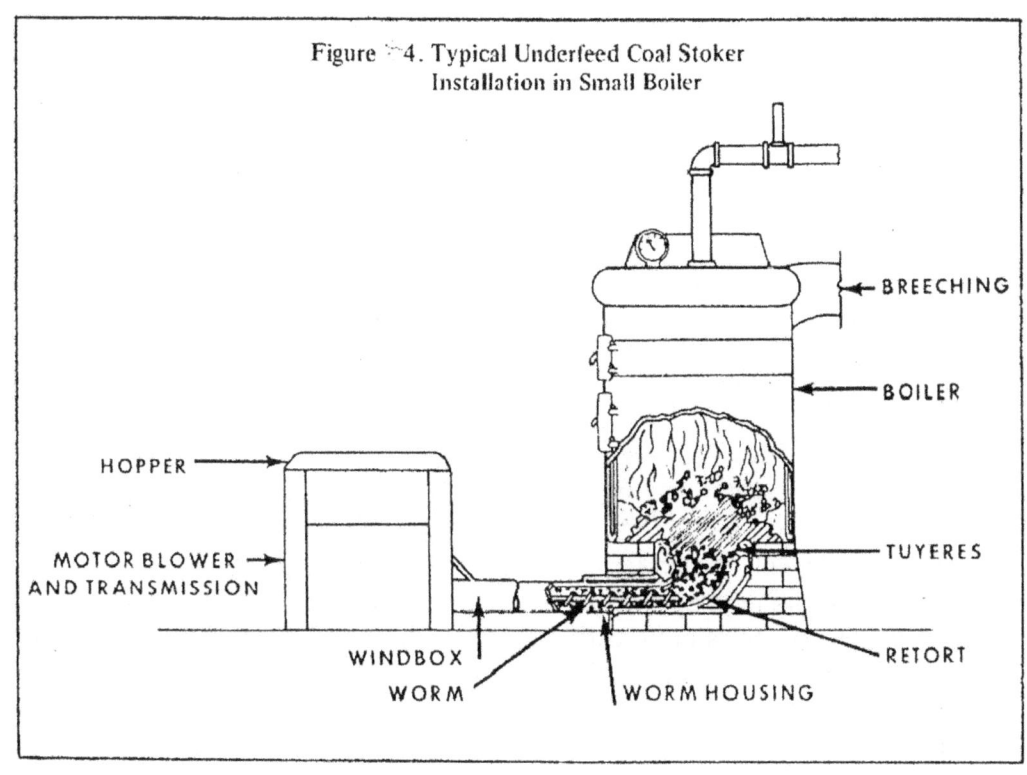

Figure 4. Typical Underfeed Coal Stoker Installation in Small Boiler

siderably in excess of this are sometimes used.

The form and parts of low-pressure air-atomizing burners (see Figure 5), are similar to high-pressure atomizing burners except for addition of a small air pump, and a different way of delivering air and oil to the nozzle or orifice.

b **Vertical rotary burners** - The atomizing-type burner, sometimes known as a radiant or suspended-flame burner, atomizes oil by throwing it from the circumference of a rapidly rotating motor-driven cup. The burner is installed so that the driving parts are protected from the heat of the flame by a hearth of refractory material at about the grate elevation. Oil is fed by pump or gravity, while the draft is mechanical or a combination of natural and mechanical.

c **Horizontal rotary burners** These were originally designed for commercial and industrial use but are available in sizes suitable for domestic use. In this burner, oil is atomized by being thrown in a

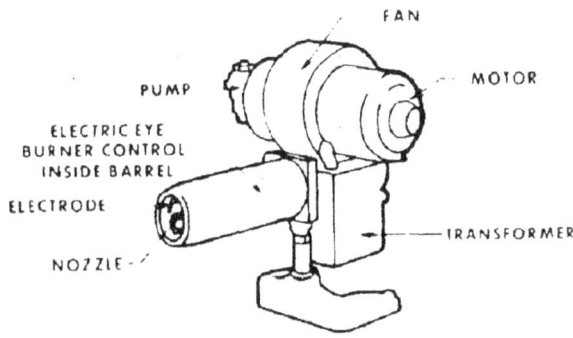

Figure 5. Cut-Away of Typical High-Pressure Gun-Burner

conical spray from a rapidly rotating cup. Horizontal rotary burners employ electric-gas or gas-pilot ignition and operate with a wide range of fuels, primarily with Numbers 1 and 2 fuel oil. Primary safety controls for burner operation are. necessary. An anti-flooding device must be a part of the system so that, if ignition in the burner should fail, the oil will not continue to flow. Likewise, a stack control is necessary to shut off the burner if the stack temperatures become excessive. A reset button on the older stack control units releases if excessive (predetermined) temperatures are exceeded and thus cuts off all power to the burner. This button must be reset before starting can be attempted. The newer models now use electric eye-type control on the burner itself.

2 **Ignition** — On the basis of the method employed to ignite fuels, burners are divided into five groups as follows:

a **Electric** — A high-voltage electric spark is made in the path of an oil and air mixture and this causes ignition. This electric spark may be continuous or may be in operation only long enough to ignite the oil. Electric ignition is almost universally used. Electrodes are located near the nozzles (see Figure 5) but not in the path of the oil spray.

b **Gas pilot** — A small gas pilot light that burns continuously is frequently used. Gas pilots usually have expanding gas valves that automatically increase flame size when motor circuit starts. After a fixed interval, the flame reverts to normal size.

c. **Electric gas** — An electric spark ignites a gas jet, which in turn ignites the oil air mixture.

d **Oil pilot** — A small oil flame is used.

e **Manual** — A burning wick or torch is placed in the combustion space through peepholes and thus ignites the charge. Operator should stand to one side of the fire door to guard against injury from chance explosion.

VI. Refractory

The refractory lining or material should be an insulating fireproof brick-like substance. Never use ordinary firebrick. The insulating brick should be set on end so as to build a 2 inch-thick wall in the pot. Size and shape of the refractory pot vary from furnace to furnace (see Figure 6 for various shapes). The shape can be either round or square, whichever is more convenient to build. It is important to use a special cement having properties similar to that of the insulating refractory-type brick.

VII. Heating Systems

A Steam Heating Systems - Steam heating systems are classified according to the pipe arrangement, accessories used, method of returning the con-densate to the boiler, method of expelling air from the system, or the type of control employed. The successful operation of a steam heating system consists of generating steam in sufficient quantity to equalize building heat loss at maximum efficiency, expelling entrapped air, and returning all condensate to the boiler rapidly. Steam cannot enter a space filled with air or water at pressure equal to the steam pressure. It is important, therefore, to eliminate air and to remove water from the distribution system. All hot pipe lines exposed to contact by residents must be properly insulated or guarded.

Steam heating systems are classified according to the method of returning the condensate to the boiler.

1 Gravity One-pipe Air-vent System — The gravity one-pipe air-vent system is one of the earliest types used. The condensate is returned to the boiler by gravity. This system is generally found in one-building-type heating systems. The steam is supplied by the boiler and carried through a single system or pipe to radiators as shown in Figure 7. Return of the condensate is dependent on hydrostatic head. Therefore, the end of the steam main, where it attaches to the boiler, must be full of water (termed a wet return) for a distance above the boiler line to create a pressure drop balance between the boiler and the steam main.

Radiators are equipped with an inlet valve and with an air valve (see Figure 8). The air valve permits venting of air from the radiator and its displacement by steam. Condensate is drained from the radiator through the same pipe that supplies steam.

2 Two-pipe Steam Vapor System with Return Trap — The two-pipe vapor system with boiler return trap and air eliminator is an improvement of the one-pipe system. The return connection of the radiator has a thermostatic trap that permits flow of condensate and air only from the radiator and prevents steam from leaving the radiator. Since the return main is at atmospheric pressure or less, a boiler return trap is installed to equalize condensate return pressure with boiler pressure.

B **Hot Water Heating Systems** — All hot water heating systems are similar in design and operating principle.

1 One-pipe Gravity System —The one-pipe gravity hot water heating system is the most elementary of the gravity systems and is shown in Figure 9. Water is heated at the lowest point in the system. It rises through a single main because of a difference in density between hot and cold water. The supply rise or radiator branch takes off from the top of the main to supply water to the radiators. After the water gives up heat in the radiator it goes back to the same main through return piping from the radiator. This cooler return water mixes with water in the supply main and causes the water to cool a little. As a result, the next radiator on the system has a lower emission rate and must be larger.

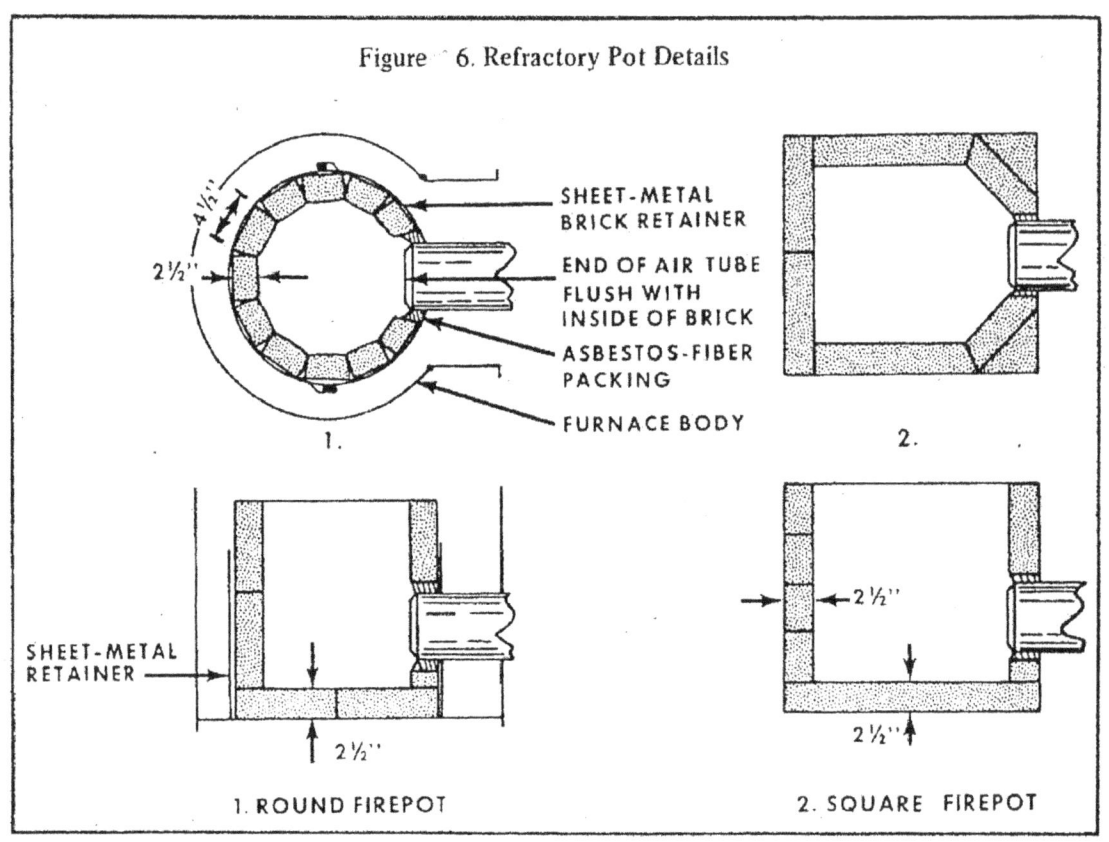

Figure 6. Refractory Pot Details

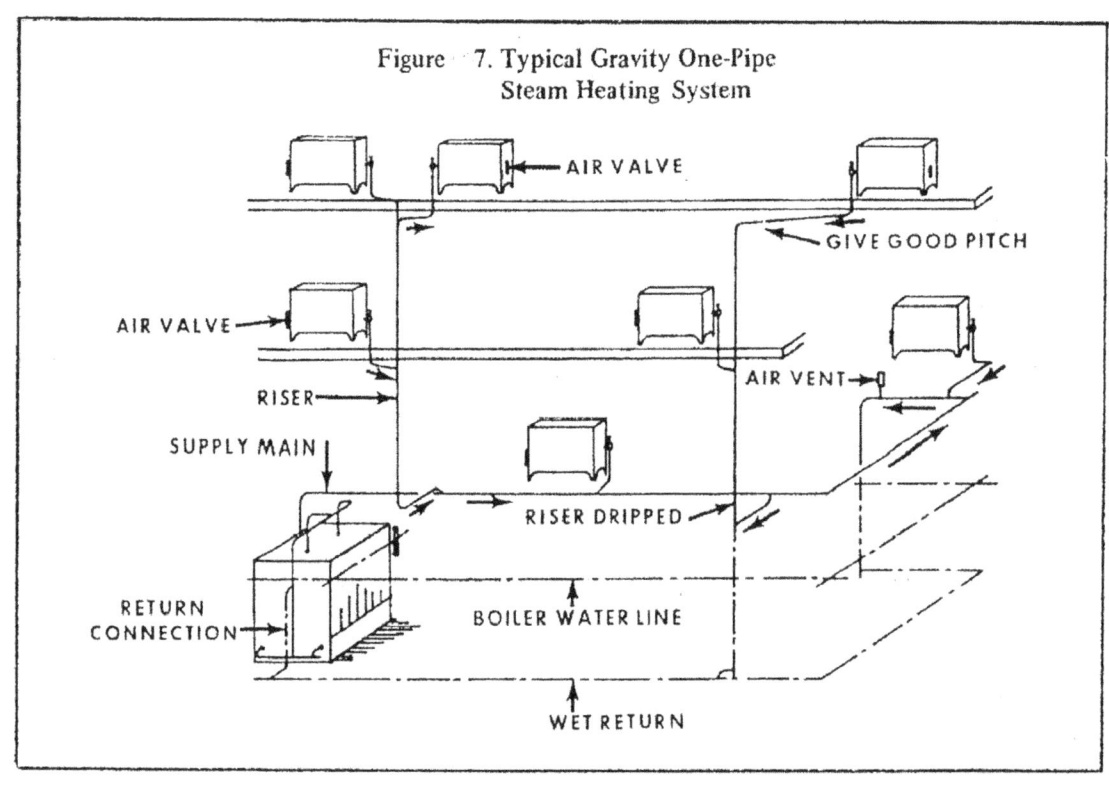

Figure 7. Typical Gravity One-Pipe Steam Heating System

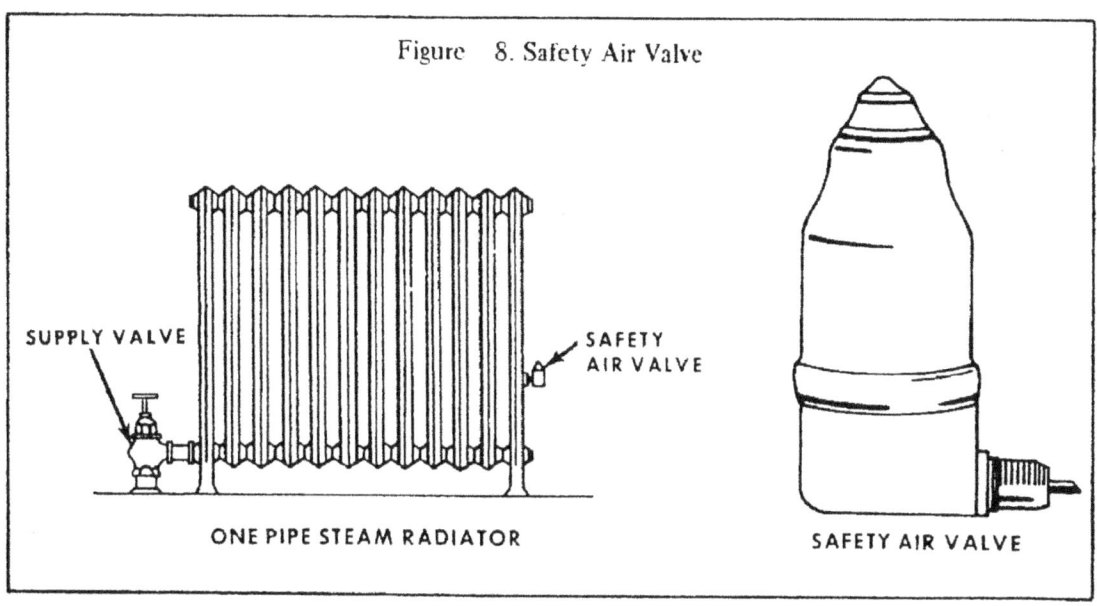

Figure 8. Safety Air Valve

Note in Figure 9 that the high points of the hot water system are vented and the low points are drained. In this case, the radiators are the high points and the heater is the low point.

2 **One-pipe Forced-feed System** — If a pump or circulator is introduced in the main near the heater of the one-pipe system, we have a forced system that can be used for much larger

applications than the gravity type. This system can operate at higher water temperatures than the gravity system. The faster moving higher temperature water "Hakes a more responsive system with a smaller temperature drop through each radiator. Higher operating temperatures and lower temperature drops permit the use of smaller radiators for the same heating load.

3 **Two-pipe Gravity Systems** — One-pipe gravity systems may become a two-pipe system if the return radiator branch connects to a second main that returns water to the heater (see Figure 10). Water temperature is practically the same in all the radiators.

4 **Two-pipe Forced-circulation System** — This system is similar to a one-pipe forced-circulation system except that the same piping arrangement is found in the two-pipe gravity flow system.

5 **Expansion Tanks** — When water is heated it tends to expand. Therefore, in a hot water system an expansion tank is necessary. The expansion tank, either of open or closed type, must be of sufficient size to permit a change in water volume within the heating system. If the expansion tank is of the open type it must be placed at least 3 feet above the highest point of the system. It will require a vent and an overflow. The open tank is usually in an attic, where it needs protection from freezing.

The enclosed expansion tank is found in modern installations. An air cushion in the tank compresses and expands according to the change of volume and pressure in the system. Closed tanks are usually at the low point in the system and close to the heater. They can, however, be placed at almost any location within the heating system.

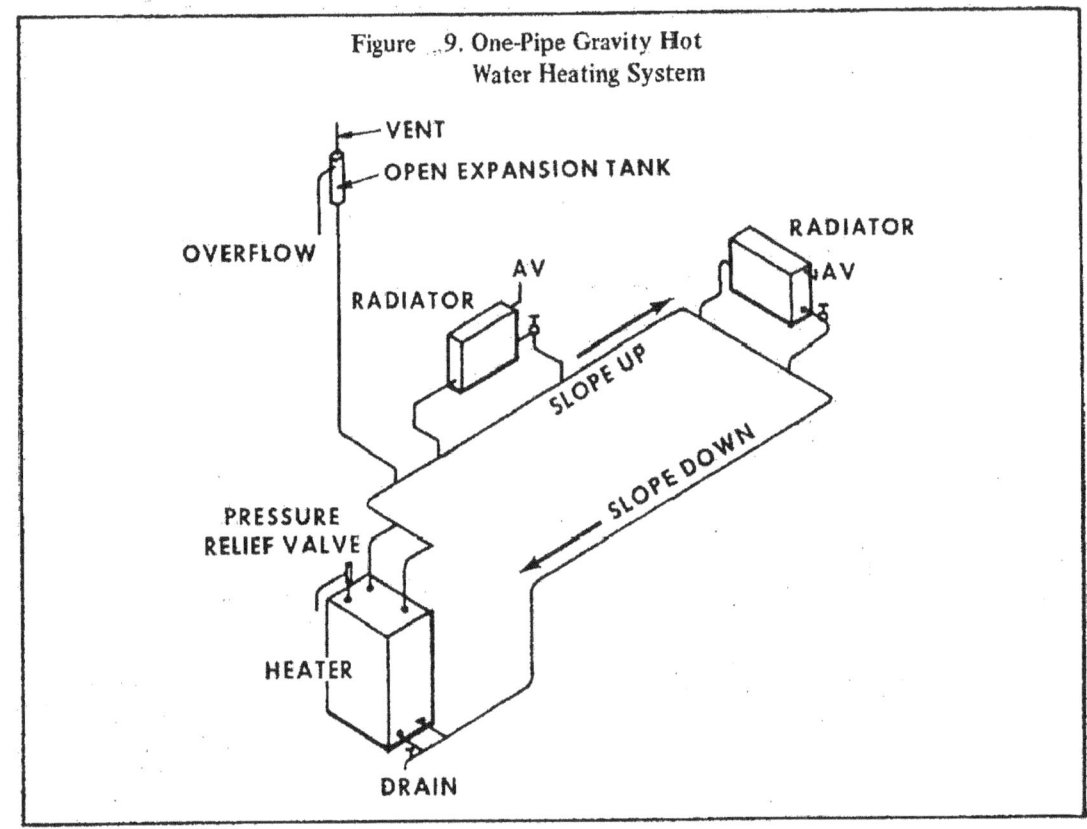

Figure 9. One-Pipe Gravity Hot Water Heating System

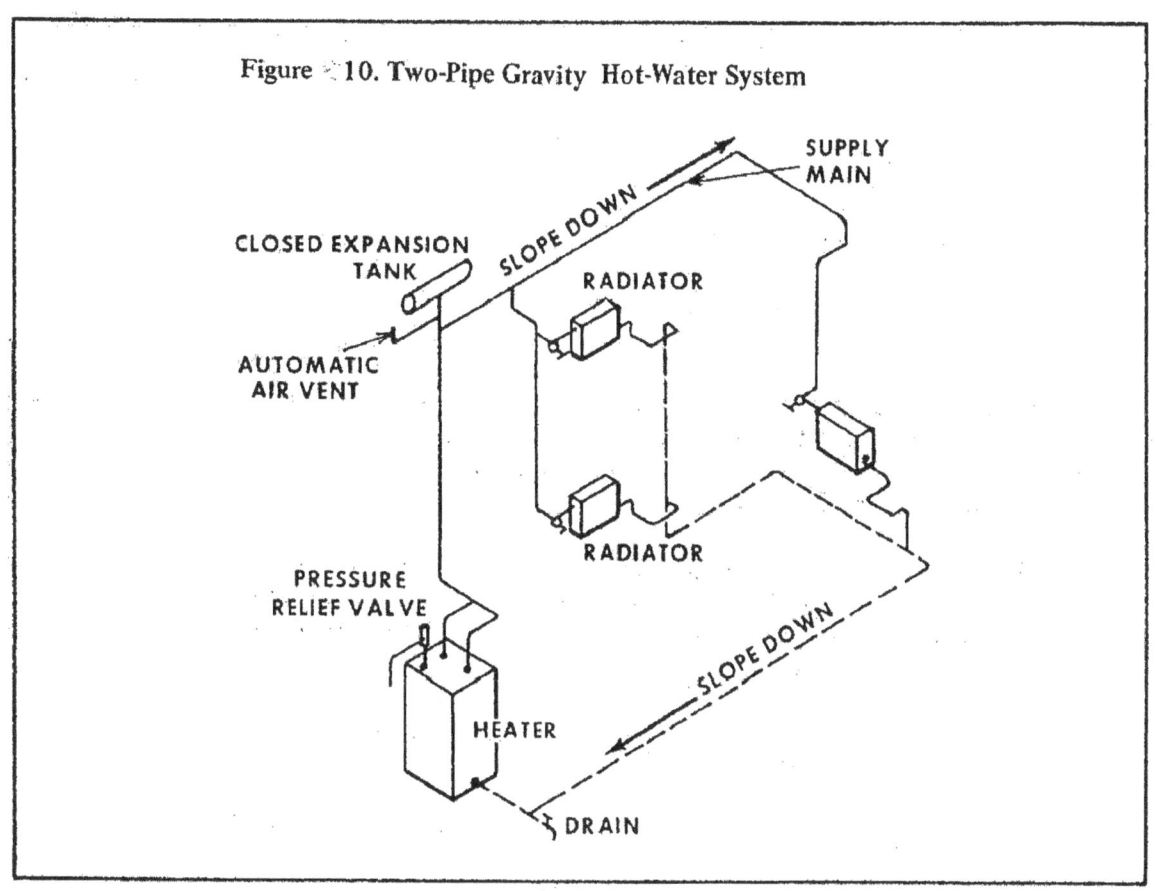

Figure 10. Two-Pipe Gravity Hot-Water System

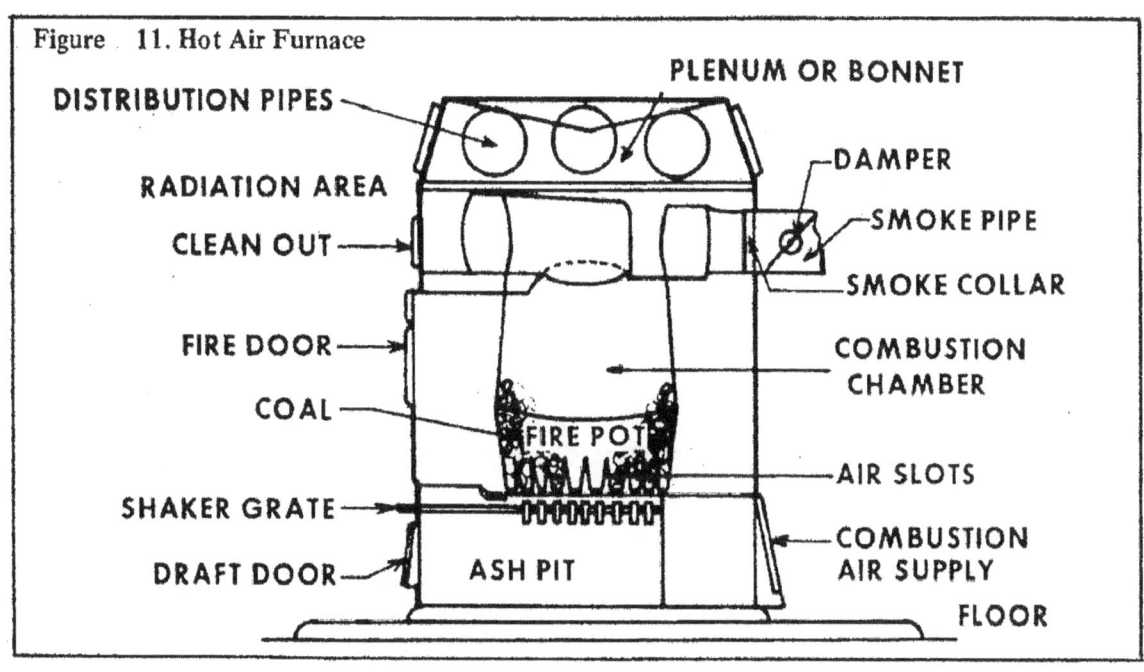

Figure 11. Hot Air Furnace

COAL NOTES

1. Approximately 12 pounds of air is required for complete combustion of 1 pound of hard coal.

2. Approximately 5 pounds of hard coal is consumed per hour for each square foot of grate area.

3. Approximately 12 inches of fire bed will heat most efficiently.

4. Anthracite coal burns more slowly than soft coal, is cleaner to handle-hence more widely used.

5. Large-size coal does not compact-hence the air spaces are too great and allows gases to escape into the flue unburned. Small size coal compacts too much and inhibits airflow through the coal to allow for good combustion. Mixing of coal size is recommended, i.e., stove and chestnut.

6. Fires burn best when the weather is clear and cold, because of reduced atmospheric pressure on the air in the flue—hence greater draft velocity. During periods of heavy atmosphere or rainy weather the temperature of flue gases must exceed normal temperatures to overcome the heavier atmospheric weight.

7. During extreme cold weather, coal should be added to a fire once in approximately 8 hours; moderate weather-12 hours.

C Hot Air Heating Systems

1 Gravity-Warm-Air Heating Systems — These operate because of the difference in specific gravity of warm air and cold air. Warm air is lighter than cold air and rises if cold air is available to replace it (see Figure 11).

a Operation — Satisfactory operation of a gravity-warm-air heating system depends on three factors. They are: (1) size of warm air and cold ducts, (2) heat loss of the building, (3) heat available from the furnace.

b Heat distribution — The most common source of trouble in these systems is insufficient pipe area usually in the return or cold air duct. The total cross-section area of the cold duct or ducts must be at least equal to the total cross-section area of all warm ducts.

c Pipeless furnaces — The pipeless hot-air furnace is the simplest type of hot-air furnace and is suitable for small homes where all rooms can be grouped about a single large register (see Figure 3). Other pipeless gravity furnaces are often installed at floor level. These are really oversized jacketed space heaters. The most common difficulty experienced with this type of furnace is supplying a return air opening of sufficient size on the floor.

2 Forced-Warm-Air Heating Systems — The mechanical warm-air furnace is the most modern type of warm-air equipment (see Figure 12). It is the safest type because it operates at low temperatures. The principle of a forced-warm-air heating system is very similar to that of the gravity system, except that a fan or blower is added to increase air movement. Because of the assistance of the fan or blower, the pitch of the ducts or leaders can be disregarded and it is therefore practical to deliver heated air in the most convenient places.

a Operation — In a forced-air system, operation of the fan or blower must be controlled by air temperature in a bonnet or by a blower control furnacestat. The blower control starts the fan or blower when the temperature reaches a certain point and turns the fan or blower off when the temperature drops to a predetermined point.

b Heat distribution — Dampers in the various warm-air ducts control distribution

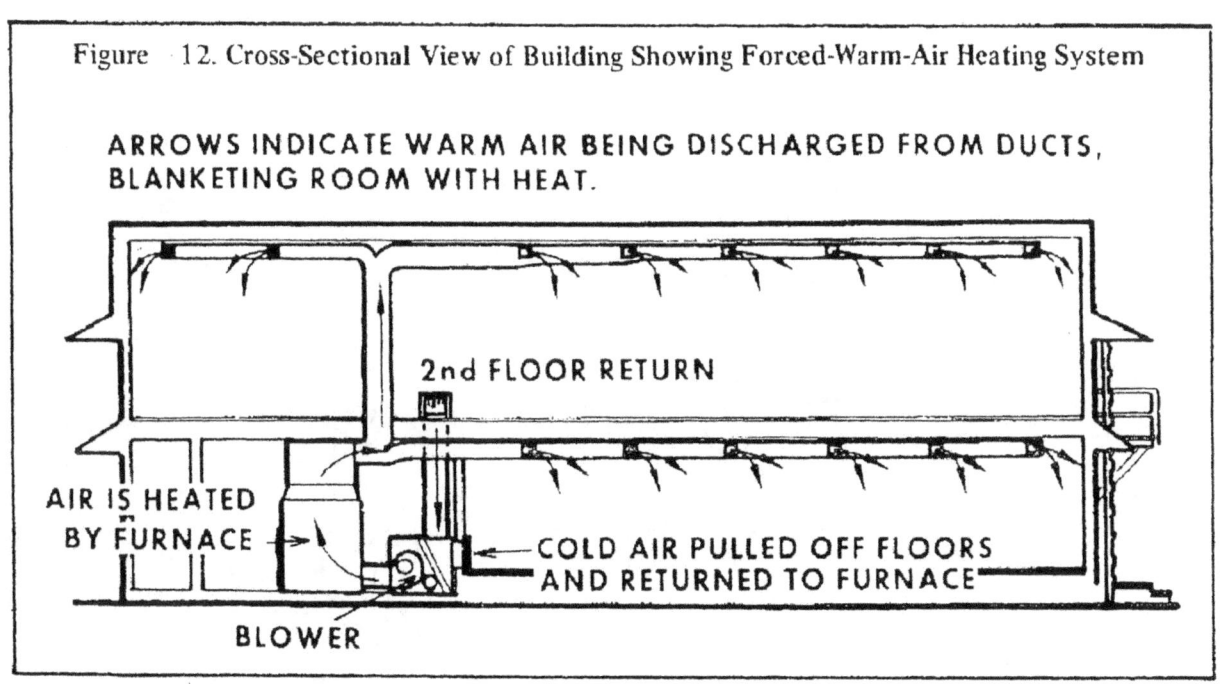

Figure 12. Cross-Sectional View of Building Showing Forced-Warm-Air Heating System

of warm air either at the branch takeoff or at the warm-air outlet.

Humidifiers are often mounted in the supply bonnet in order to regulate the humidity within the residence.

D Space Heaters — Space unit heaters are the least desirable from the viewpoint of fire safety and housing inspection. All space unit heaters must be vented to the flue.

1 Coal-Fired Space Heaters (Cannon stove) — This is illustrated in Figure 13 and is made entirely of cast iron. In operation, coal on the grates receives primary air for combustion through the grates from the ash-door draft intake. Combustible gases driven from the coal by heat burn in the barrel of the stove, where they received additional or secondary air through the feed door. Side and top of the stove absorb the heat of combustion and radiate it to the surrounding space.

2 Oil-Fired Space Heaters — Oil-fired space heaters have atmospheric vaporizing-type burners. The burners require a light grade of fuel oil that vaporizes easily and is comparatively low in temperature. In addition, the oil must be such that it leaves only a small amount of carbon residue and ash within the heater. Oil-fired space heaters are basically of two types:

a Perforated-sleeve burner — The perforated-sleeve burner (see Figure 14) consists essentially of a metal base formed of two or more angular fuel-vaporizing bowl burners (see Figure 15) and is widely used in space heaters and some water heaters.

The burner consists essentially of a bowl, 8 to 13 inches in diameter, with perforations in the side that admit air for combustion. The upper part of the bowl has a flame ring or collar. When several space heaters are installed in a building, an oil supply from an

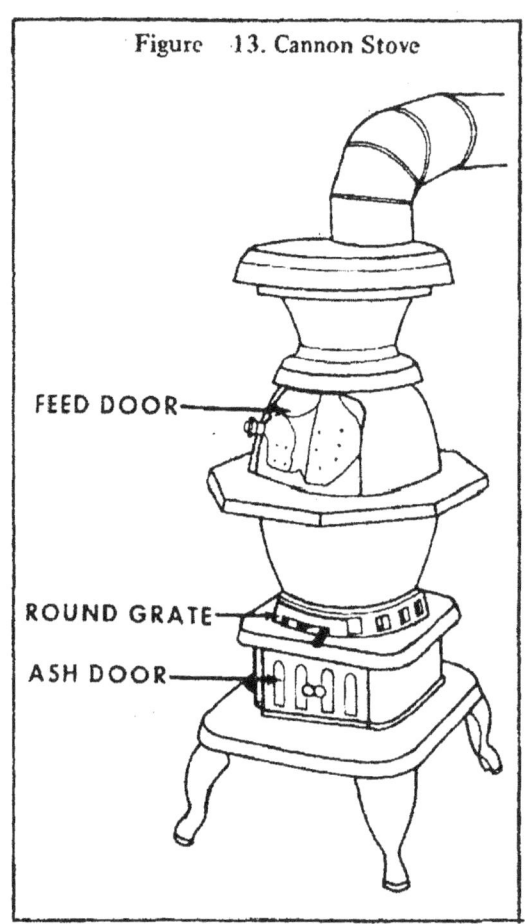

Figure 13. Cannon Stove

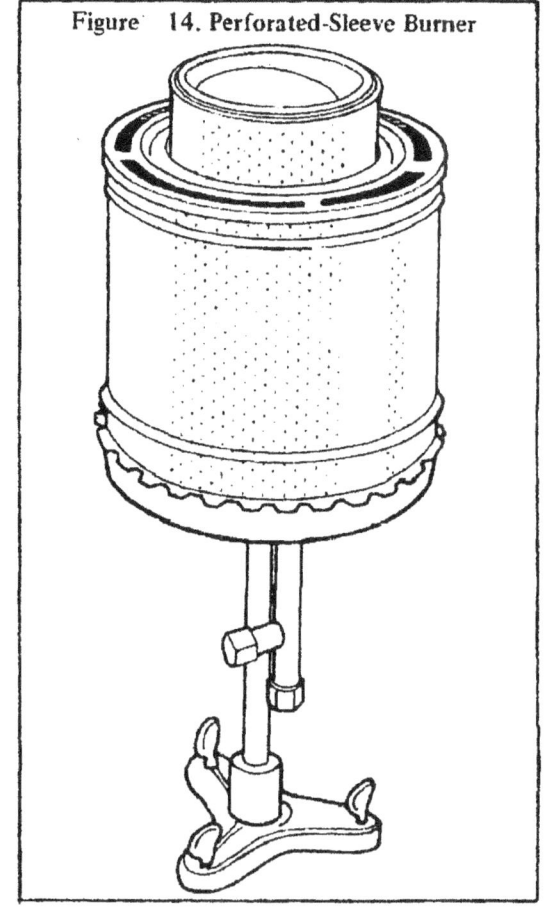

Figure 14. Perforated-Sleeve Burner

outside tank to all heaters is often desirable. Figure 16 shows the condition of a burner flame with different rates of fuel flow and indicates the ideal flame height.

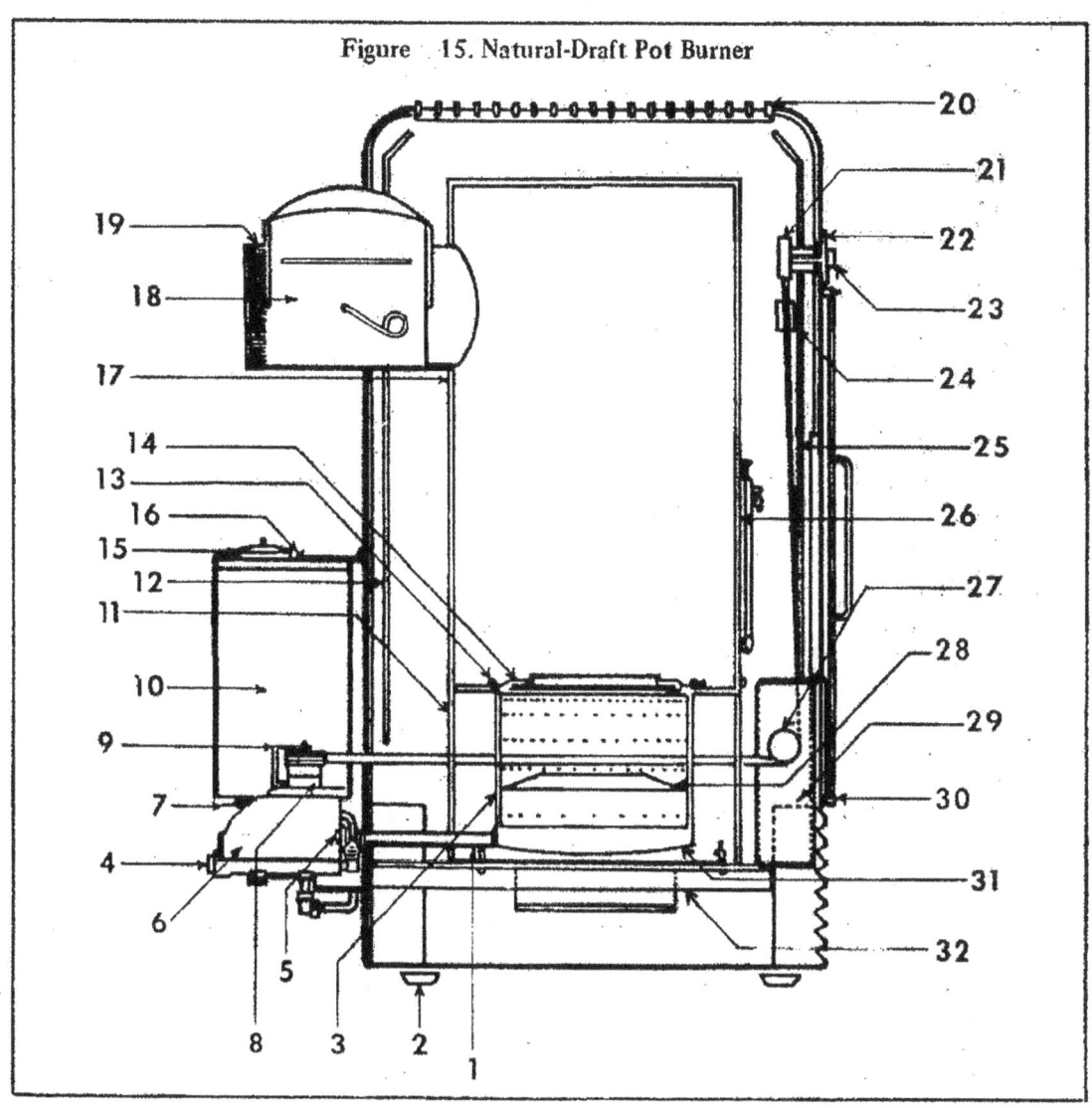

Figure 15. Natural-Draft Pot Burner

1 Burner-pot pipe.
2 Leg Leveler.
3 Pilot-ring clip.
4 Strainer unit.
5 Burner-pot drain plug.
6 Constant-level valve.
7 Tank valve
8 Control drum (to fit 6).
9 Control pulley bracket
10 Fuel tank.
11 Lower heat unit.
12 Heat shield (rear).
13 Burner-ring clamp.
14 Burner-top ring.
15 Fuel tank cap.
16 Tank fuel gauge.
17 Heat unit.
18 Cold draft regulator.
19 Flue connections, 6-inch diameter.
20 Top grille.
21 Dial control drum.
22 Escutcheon plate.
23 Dial control knob.
24 Pulley assembly (short).
25 Heat shield (front).
26 Heat-unit door.
27 Pulley assembly (long).
28 Pilot ring.
29 Humidifier.
30 Trim bar.
31 Burner pot.
32 Heat-unit support.

3 Gas-Fired Space Heaters—There are three types of gas-fired space heaters: natural, manufactured, and liquified petroleum gas. Space heaters using natural, manufactured, or liquified petroleum gases have a similar construction. All gas-fired space heaters must be vented to prevent a dangerous buildup of poisonous gases.

Each unit console consists of an enamel steel cabinet with top and bottom circulating grilles or openings, gas burners, heating element, gas pilot, and gas valve (see Figure 17). The heating element or combustion chamber is usually cast iron.

CAUTION: All gas-fired space heaters and their connections must be of the type approved by the American Gas Association (AGA). They must be installed in accordance with the recommendations of that organization or the local code.

a Venting — Use of proper venting materials and correct installation of venting for gas-fired space heaters is necessary to minimize harmful effects of condensation and to ensure that combustion products are carried off. (Approximately 12 gallons of water are produced in the burning of 1,000 cubic feet of natural gas. The inner surface of the vent must therefore be heated above the dewpoint of the combustion products to prevent water from forming in the flue.) A horizontal vent must be given an upward pitch of at least 1 inch per foot of horizontal distance.

When the smoke pipe extends through floors or walls the metal pipe must be insu-

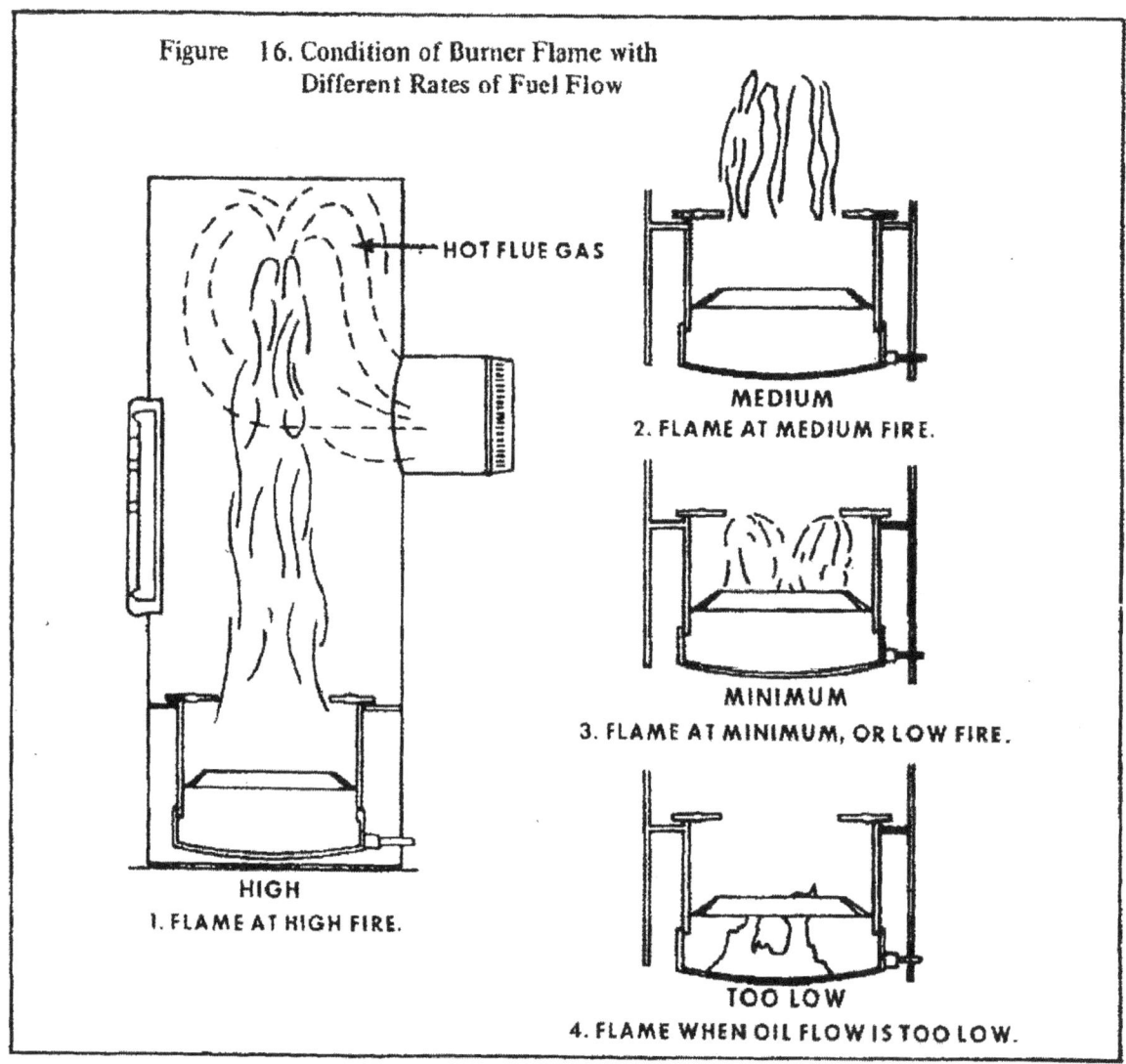

Figure 16. Condition of Burner Flame with Different Rates of Fuel Flow

lated from the floor or wall system by an air space (see Figure 18). Avoid sharp bends. A 90° vent elbow has a resistance to flow equivalent to a straight section of pipe having a length of 10 times the elbow diameter. Be sure vent is of a rigid construction and resistant to corrosion by flue gas products. Several types of venting material are available such as B-vent and several other ceramic-type materials. A chimney lined with fire-brick type of terra cotta must be relined with an acceptable vent material if it is to be used for venting gas-fired appliances.

Use the same size vent pipe throughout its length. Never make a vent smaller than heater outlet except when two or more vents converge from separate heaters. To determine the size of vents beyond the point of convergence, add one-half the area of each vent to the area of the largest heater's vent.

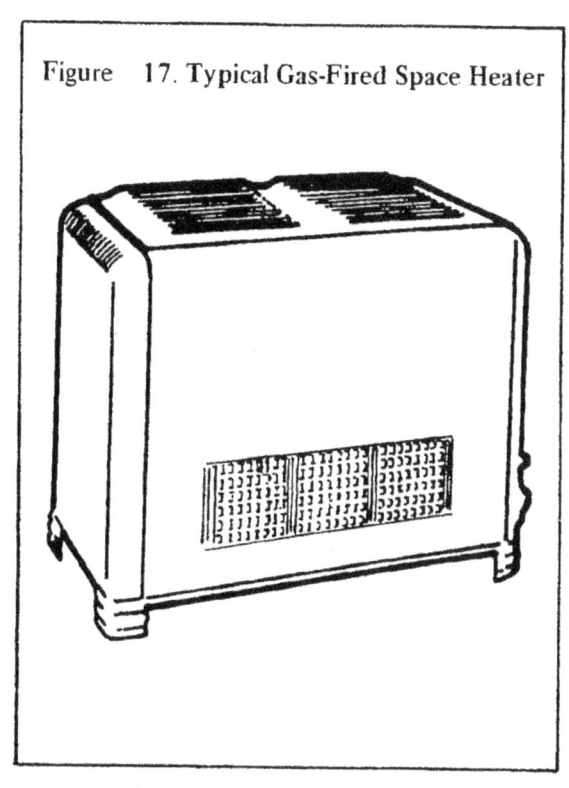

Figure 17. Typical Gas-Fired Space Heater

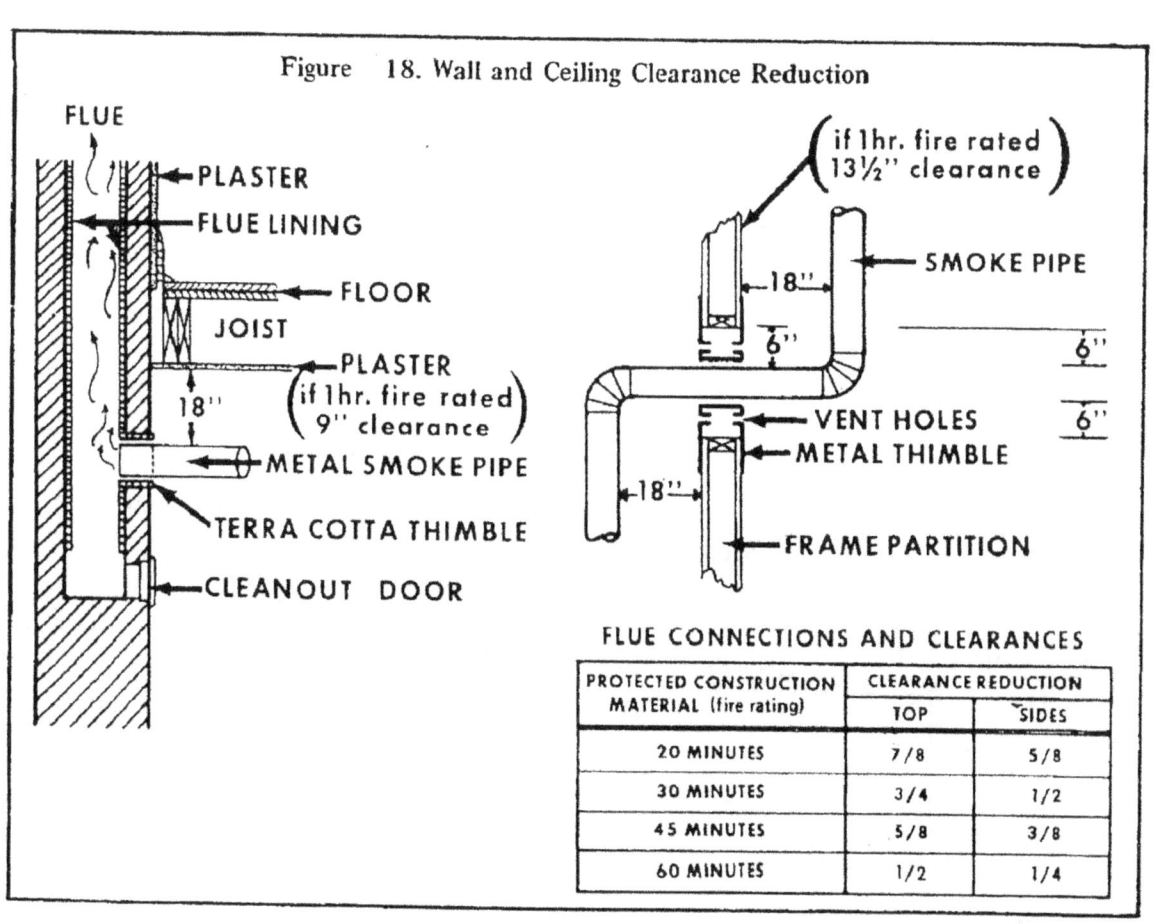

Figure 18. Wall and Ceiling Clearance Reduction

FLUE CONNECTIONS AND CLEARANCES

PROTECTED CONSTRUCTION MATERIAL (fire rating)	CLEARANCE REDUCTION	
	TOP	SIDES
20 MINUTES	7/8	5/8
30 MINUTES	3/4	1/2
45 MINUTES	5/8	3/8
60 MINUTES	1/2	1/4

Install vents with male ends of inner liner down to ensure condensate is kept within pipes on a cold start. The vertical length of each vent or stack should be at least 2 feet greater than the length between horizontal connection and stack.

Run vent at least 3 feet above any projection of the building within 20 feet to place it above a possible pressure zone due to wind currents (see Figure 19). End it with a weather cap designed to prevent entrance of rain and snow.

Gas-fired space heaters as well as gas furnaces and hot water heaters must be equipped with a backdraft diverter (see Figure ,20) designed to protect heaters against downdrafts and excessive updrafts. Use only draft diverters of the type approved by the AGA.

The combustion chamber or firebox must be insulated from the floor, usually with an airspace of 15 to 18 inches, or the firebox is sometimes insulated within the unit and thus allows for lesser clearance for combustibles.

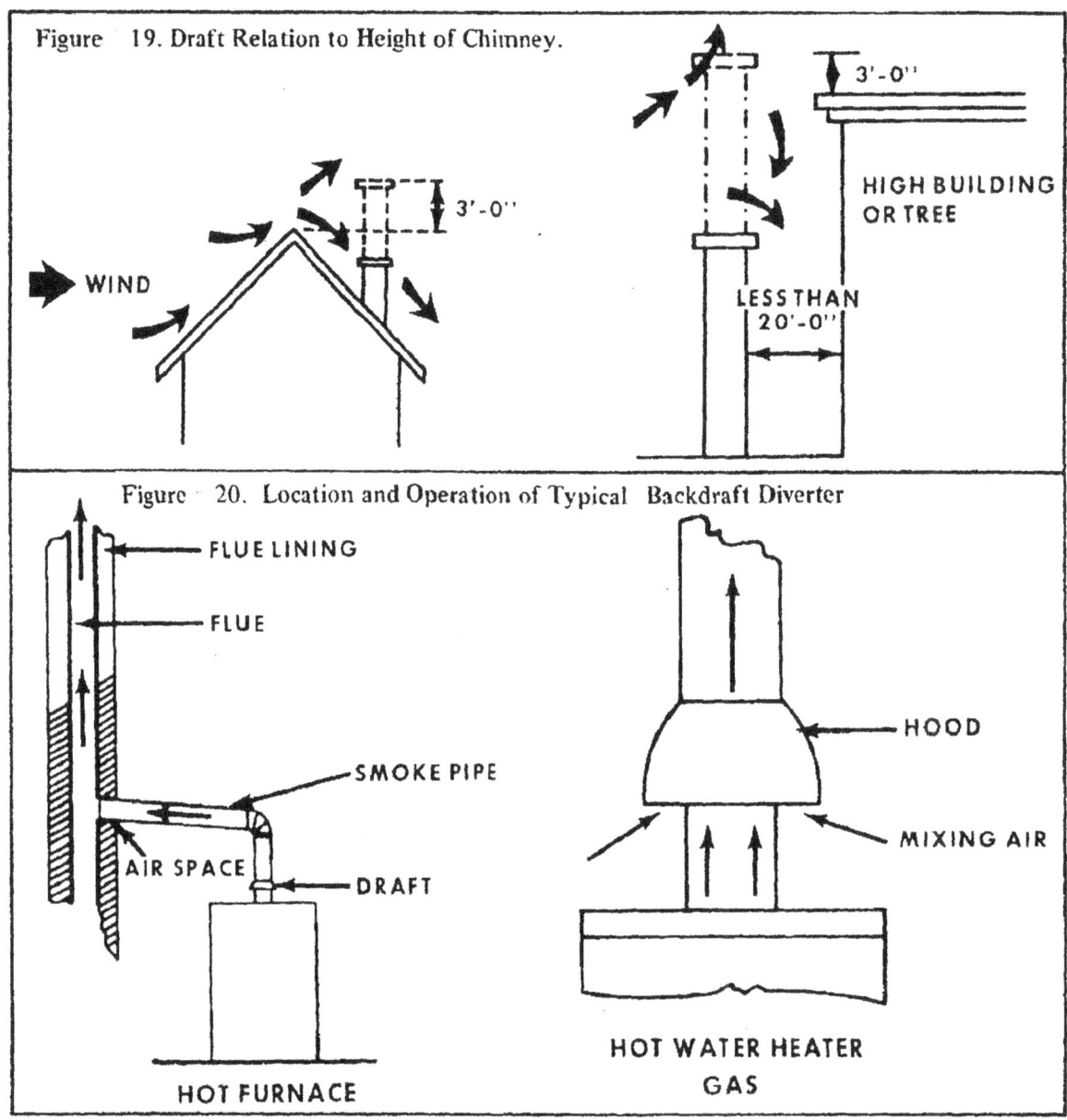

Figure 19. Draft Relation to Height of Chimney.

Figure 20. Location and Operation of Typical Backdraft Diverter

Where coal space heaters are located, a floor protection should be provided. This would be a metal-covered asbestos board or a similar durable insulation material. One reason for the floor protection would be to allow cooling off of hot coals and ashes if they drop out while ashes are being removed from the ash chamber. Walls and ceilings of a non-combustible construction exposed to furnace radiation should be installed, and the following clearances are recommended: Space heaters — A top or ceiling clearance of 36 inches, a wall clearance of 18 inches, and a smoke pipe clearance of 18 inches, (see Figure 18).

VIII. Domestic Hot Water Jack Stoves (Coal Stoves)

Domestic hot water jack stoves (coal stoves) equipped with water jackets to supply hot water for domestic use are to be treated as coal-fired furnaces or boilers previously discussed. Note that flue connections should not exceed two to the same flue unless the draft and size are sufficient to accommodate both exhausting requirements. One flue with one smoke pipe is the rule; however, housing inspectors may find a jack stove and main furnace connected to the same flue. Where these conditions are encountered and no complaint about malfunctioning of this system is found, it can be assumed that the system is operating satisfactorily. Where more than two units, other than gas, are attached to a single flue, the building agency should be notified, since this can be considered an improper installation. Gas, oil, and electric hot water heating units for domestic hot water should be treated the same as previously discussed for central heating units.

IX. Hazardous Installations

A **Generalities** — The housing inspector should be on the alert for unvented open burning flame heaters, such as manually operated gas logs. Coil-type wall-mounted hot-water heaters that do not have safety relief valves are not permitted. Kerosene (portable) units for cooking or heating should be prohibited. Generally, open-flame portable units are not allowed under fire safety regulations.

In oil heating units, other than integral tank units, the oil filling and vent must be located on the exterior of the building. Filling of oil within buildings is prohibited.

Electric wiring to heating units must be installed as indicated in the electrical section. Cutoff switches should be close to the entry but outside of the boiler room. The inspector should be able to appraise the heating installation and determine its adequacy. Any installation that indicates haphazard location, workmanship, or operation, whether it be building, zoning, plumbing, electrical, or housing, will dictate further inspection.

B **Chimneys (see Figure 21 and 22)** - Chimneys, as all inspectors know, are an integral part of the building. The chimney is a point of building safety and should be understood by the housing inspector. The chimney, if of masonry, must be tight and sound; flues should be terra cotta lined, and where no linings are installed, the brick should be tight to permit proper draft and elimination of combustion gases.

Chimneys that act as flues for gas-fired equipment must be lined with either B-vent or terra cotta.

To the inspector, on exterior inspection, "banana peel" on the portion of the chimney above the roof will indicate trouble and a need for rebuilding. Exterior deterioration of the chimney will, if let go too long, gradually permit erosion from within the flues and eventually block the flue opening.

Rusted flashing at the roof level will also contribute to the chimney's deterioration. Effervescence on the inside wall of the chimney below the roof and on the outside of the chimney, if exposed, will show salt accumulations — a tell-tale sign of water penetration and flue gas escape and a sign of chimney deterioration. In the spring and fall, during rain seasons, if terra cotta chimneys leak, the joint will be indicated by dark areas permitting actual counting of the number of flues inside the masonry chimney. When this condition occurs, it usually requires 2 or 3 months to dry out. Upon drying out, the mortar joints are discolored (brown), and so after a few years of this type of deterioration the joints can be distinguished wet or dry. The above-listed conditions usually develop during coal operation and become more pronounced usually 2 to 5 years after conversion to oil or gas.

An unlined chimney can be checked for deterioration below the roof line by checking the residue deposited at the base of the chimney, usually accessible through a cleanout (door or plug) or breaching. Red granular or fine powder showing through coal soot or oil soot will generally indicate, if in quantity (a handful), that deterioration is excessive and repairs are needed.

Gas units attached to unlined chimneys will be devoid of soot, but will usually show similar tell-tale brick powder and deterioration as previously mentioned. Manufactured gas has a greater tendency to dehydrate and decompose brick in chimney flues than natural gas. For gas installations in older homes, utility companies usually specify chimney requirements before installation, and so older chimneys may require the installation of terra cotta liners, lead-lined copper liners, or transite pipe. Oil burner operation using a low air ratio and high oil consumption is usually indicated by black carbon deposits around the top of the chimney. Prolonged operation in this burner setting results in long carbon water deposits down the chimney for 4 to 6 feet or more and should indicate to the inspector a possibility of poor burner maintenance. This will accent his need to be more thorough on the ensuing inspection. This type of condition can result from other related causes, such as improper chimney height or exterior obstructions such as trees or buildings that will cause downdrafts or insufficient draft or contribute to a faulty heating operation.

Rust spots and soot-mold usually occur on galvanized smoke pipe deterioration.

C Fireplace — Careful attention should be given to the construction of the fireplace. Improperly built fireplaces are a serious safety and fire hazard (see Figure 22). The most common causes of fireplace fires are thin walls, combustible materials such as studding or trim against sides and back of the fireplace, wood mantels, and unsafe hearths.

Fireplace walls should be not less than 0 inches thick, and if built of stone or hollow masonry units, not less than 12 inches thick. The faces of all walls exposed to fire should be lined with firebrick or other suitable fire-resistive material. When the lining consists of 4 inches of firebrick, such lining thickness may be included in the required minimum thickness of the wall.

The fireplace hearth should be constructed of brick, stone, tile, or similar incombustible material and should be supported on a fireproof slab or on a brick arch. The hearth should extend at least 20 inches beyond the chimney breast and not less than 12 inches beyond each side of the fireplace opening

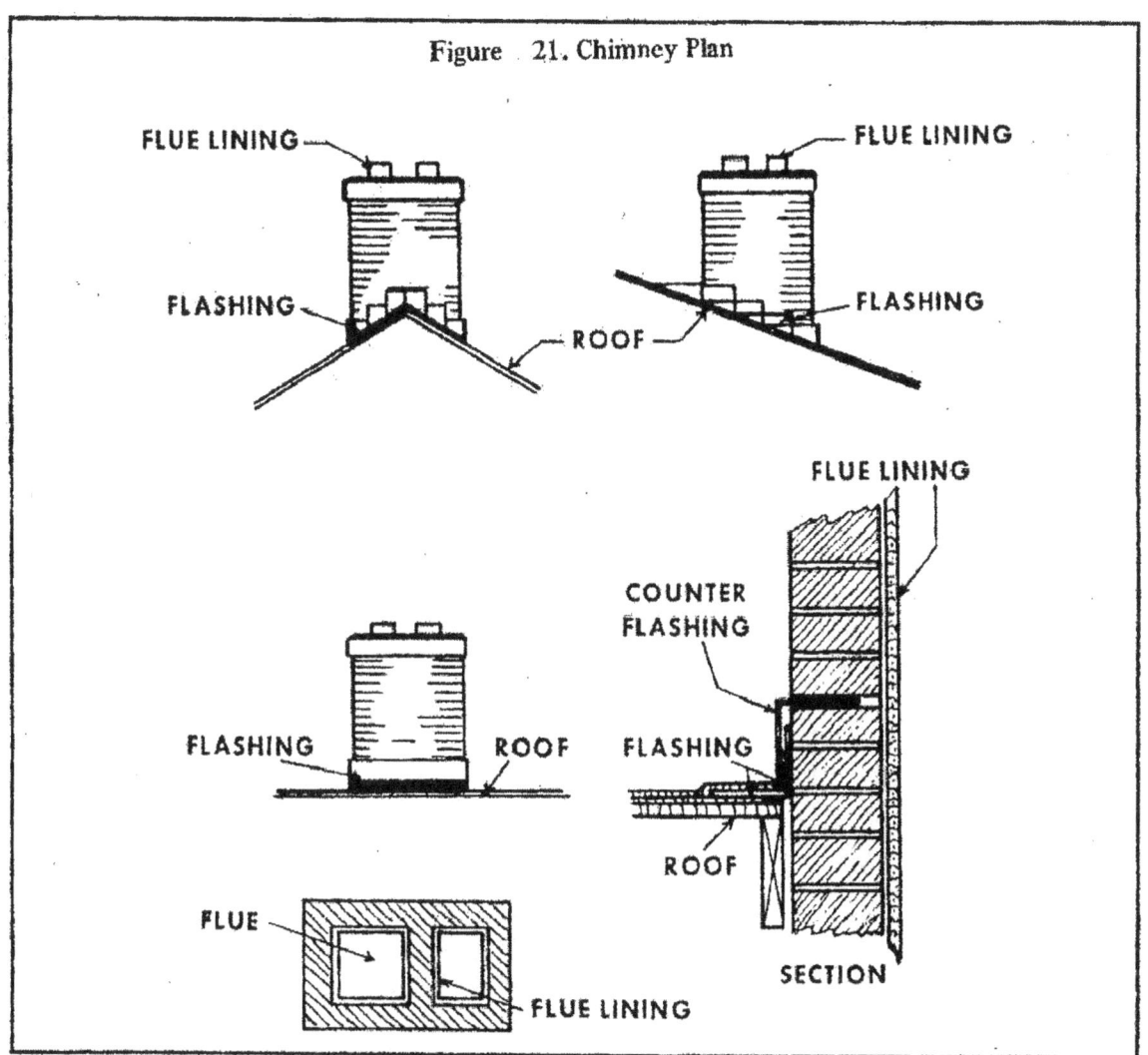

Figure 21. Chimney Plan

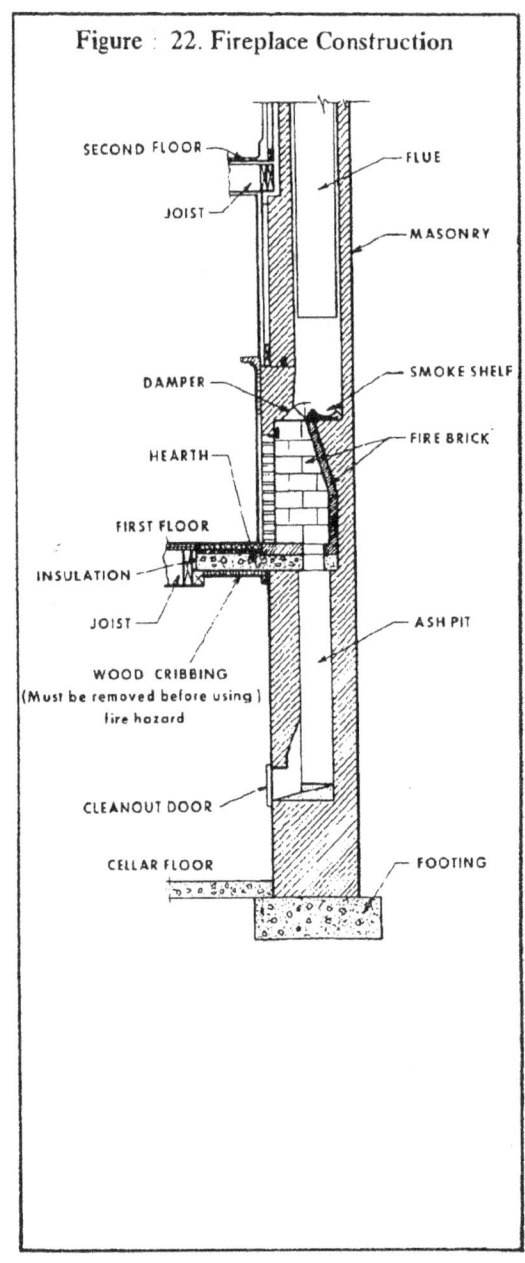

Figure 22. Fireplace Construction

along the chimney breast. The combined thickness of the hearth and its supporting construction should be not less than 6 inches at any point.

It is important that all wooden beams, joists, and studs are set off from the fireplace and chimney so that there is not less than 2 inches of clearance between the wood members and the sidewalls of the fireplace or chimney and not less than 4 inches of clearance between wood members and the back wall of the fireplace.

The housing inspector is a very important person in maintaining sound, safe, and healthful community growth. This should be a challenge to every inspector to provide himself with the necessary tools for better and more efficient housing inspection. He must develop the extra senses so necessary in spotting and correcting faults. He must know when to refer and to whom the referral is to be made; he must be continually seeking knowledge, which may be found by consulting with technicians, tradesmen, and professionals. No finer satisfaction can be realized than to know and feel that the security, safety, and comfort of each and every family within your community has a better and more healthful life because of that extra bit of knowledge you have imparted. "An inspector who stops learning today is uneducated tomorrow."

THEORY OF HEAT

CONTENTS

		Page
A.	INTRODUCTION	1
B.	MEASUREMENT OF HEAT	1
C.	KINDS OF HEAT	2
D.	PRESSURE	4
E.	VAPORIZATION	6
F.	PHYSICAL CONDITIONS OF VAPORS AND LIQUIDS	7
G.	EXPANSION AND CONTRACTION OF SUBSTANCE	7
H.	HEAT TRANSFER	8
I.	INSULATION	9

THEORY OF HEAT

A. INTRODUCTION

A1. General.—As mentioned earlier, heat is a very relative term. Usually one thinks of it as a means of warming the body, or some object, to a desired temperature. Strange as it may seem, heat is ever present, even in a block of ice. In this chapter, heat is explained in terms of how it is used and transferred from substance to substance. Heat transfer is what all refrigeration systems are designed to accomplish. To understand the basic principles of refrigeration, it is most important that the student have a definite understanding of the relationship of heat, temperatures, and pressures.

A2. Matter Defined.—Matter is anything that has weight and occupies space. All substances are forms of matter in one of three stages: solid, liquid, or gaseous. An example of a substance in its three stages is water.

In its natural state water is a liquid. It has weight, volume, and takes the shape of the container which holds it. If it is heated in a closed container to its boiling point and more heat is added, it changes to steam or vapor which is its gaseous state. It has weight and occupies the volume or space of the container. When water is frozen, it becomes ice or is in its solid state. In this state, it has weight and volume, and it takes a definite shape.

Theoretically, all substances can be converted from one to another of the three states by the addition or withdrawal of heat. However, chemical compounds differ in the ease or difficulty with which they may be changed from one to another of the three physical states. Some, like water, can very readily be converted into each of the three states; others, like paper, oxidize, or burn, at high temperatures and cannot be converted into all three. Before paper burns, it changes to a gas, but never to a liquid. The science of refrigeration depends upon changes in physical state through heating or cooling.

A3. Definition of Heat.—Heat is a form of energy. It cannot be seen or shaped, nor can it be created or destroyed. It can only be transferred from substance to substance.

All substances are made up of tiny molecules. These molecules are in constant motion and moving against each other. As the temperature of these molecules increases, so does their activity, and as heat is taken away their activity and temperature decrease. If all heat is extracted from a substance (absolute zero temperature), the molecular motion will become dormant.

B. MEASUREMENT OF HEAT

B1. Intensity and Quantity.—From experience we know that heat and temperature are related. If heat is added to a substance the temperature of the substance will rise, and if heat is taken away the temperature will decrease. There is a difference, however, in quantity and intensity. Heat is measured (1) by its intensity, and (2) by the quantity of it possessed by a substance. This is readily understood by comparing a spoonful of hot water with a pailful of warm water. The hot water in the spoon has a greater intensity of heat, but the warm water in the pail possesses a larger quantity of heat, though at a lower intensity.

B2. Thermometer.—Intensity of heat is measured by the ordinary thermometer with which everyone is familiar. The two methods of dividing and numbering the thermometer scales in common use are the Fahrenheit and the Centigrade. Another scale not so common but used by scientists is the Kelvin.

B3. Fahrenheit Scale.—The temperature scale most commonly used in refrigeration is the Fahrenheit scale represented by the designator °F. This scale is fixed to divide the difference between melting ice and boiling water into 180 equal degrees. The melting ice is represented by a mark of 32° F, and boiling water at 212° F. Degrees above and below these are also equal divisions shown on the scale. When reaching the temperature where all molecular action in all substances ceases, a thermometer reading of -459.69° F would be indicated. This is called absolute zero. Scientists have been able, under controlled conditions, to measure temperatures within a few thousandths of absolute zero.

B4. **Centigrade Scale.**—The centigrade thermometer is scaled in degrees and indicated by °C. On this scale, ice melts at 0° C and water boils at 100° C. The 100 degrees between melting point and boiling point are equally divided on the scale. The absolute zero temperature on the centigrade scale is -273.16° C.

The centigrade scaled thermometer is used in most countries except the United States and Britain. It is used universally in scientific work.

B5. **Absolute or Kelvin Scale.**—The Kelvin scale is graduated in degrees starting at zero. On this scale, 0° K is equal to -273° C or -460° F, or absolute zero. The boiling point of water, 373° K, and the melting point of ice, 273° K, are equal to readings on the Fahrenheit and centigrade scales as shown in figure 1.

B6. **British Thermal Unit.**—The quantity of heat possessed by a substance is measured in terms of the British thermal unit, abbreviated Btu. A Btu is the quantity of heat required to raise the temperature of one pound of pure water one degree Fahrenheit at or near 39.10° F. This is the temperature at which water is at maximum density. For example, to raise the temperature of five pounds of water from 39° to 49° F, or from 160° to 170° F, requires 5 x 10 = 50 Btu. For all practical purposes, the Btu is considered constant between 32° and 212° F, though it does vary a slight amount.

C. KINDS OF HEAT

C1. **General.**—To have an understanding of the terminology used in refrigeration and air conditioning, it is essential that the meaning of the terms discussed in this section be known. Some terms seem closely related, but the meaning and way they are applied is very important. The terms considered here apply to heat.

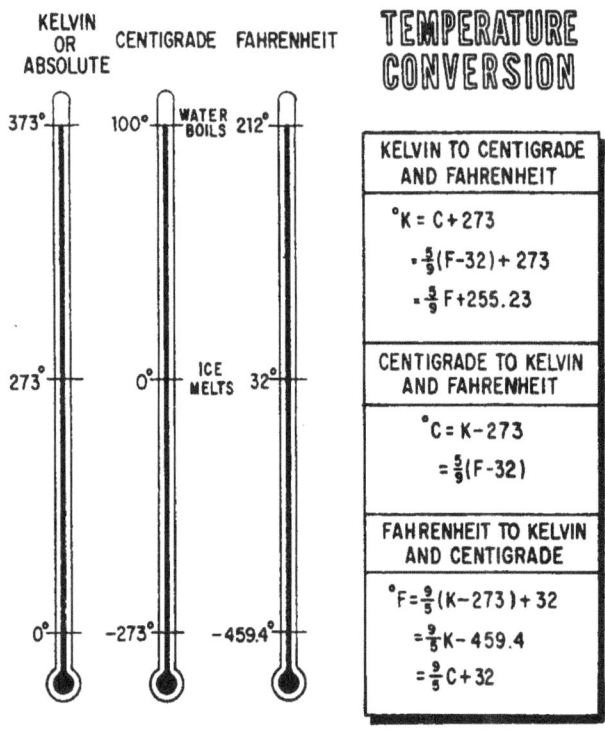

Figure 1.—Comparison of Fahrenheit, centigrade, and Kelvin temperature scales.

C2. **Specific Heat.**—Specific heat is the number of Btu that must be added to a unit weight of substance to raise its temperature 1 degree Fahrenheit. Since most substances held to a constant weight vary in volume, varying numbers of Btu are required to change the temperature 1 degree Fahrenheit per unit.

Technically, the specific heat of a substance is the ratio of the amount of heat required to change the temperature of a unit weight of that substance 1 degree to the amount of heat required to change the temperature of the same weight of water one degree. Since the specific heat of water is, by definition, equal to 1, the specific heat of other substances are expressed as decimals. Examples of the specific heat of some substances follow:

Material	Specific Heat (Btu/Lb)
Wood	.327
Ice	.504
Iron	.129
Copper	.095
Glass	.187

Mercury	.033
Alcohol	.615
Liquid Ammonia at 40° F.	1.100

C3. Thermal Capacity.—Thermal capacity is closely related to specific heat. The specific heat of a substance is the number of Btu necessary to raise the temperature of one pound of the substance one degree Fahrenheit. The thermal capacity of a substance is the amount of heat required to raise the temperature of its whole mass one degree. Hence, thermal capacity equals the specific heat of a substance multiplied by its mass. Thermal capacity may be said to express the total capacity of a given quantity of a substance for absorbing and storing heat. Thermal capacity is stated, not as a ratio, but as a certain number of Btu.

C4. Sensible Heat.—Heat that is added to, or subtracted from, a substance that changes its temperature but not its physical state is called sensible heat. It is the heat that can be indicated on a thermometer. This is the heat which human senses also can react to, at least within certain ranges. For example, if a person puts his finger into a cup of water, his senses readily tell him whether it is cold, cool, tepid, hot, or very hot. Human senses are not sufficiently discriminating to give precise information about the extreme temperatures of ice and steam or other substances having temperatures beyond the range of human sensory mechanisms. Ice merely seems cold and steam seems hot whatever their temperatures. Sensible heat is applied to a solid (as ice), a liquid (as water), or a vapor/gas (as steam) as indicated on a thermometer. The term sensible heat does not apply to the process of conversion from one physical state to another.

C5. Latent Heat.—Heat absorbed, or given up, during the conversion of a substance from one physical state to another has another name. This is called latent heat. The term, latent heat, has two forms; latent heat of fusion and latent heat of vaporization.

Latent is taken from the Greek language meaning hidden. When latent heat is added to or subtracted from a substance, and the physical change takes place, there is no change in the sensible heat or temperature of the substance.

C6. Latent Heat of Fusion.—If heat is applied to a piece of ice at a temperature of 0° F, the temperature of the ice would gradually rise. This change in temperature, which can be indicated by placing a thermometer on the ice, is called sensible heat as stated previously. No change in state takes place, only a change in the temperature of the ice.

As more sensible heat is added, the temperature of the ice finally reaches 32° F. Now, as more heat is absorbed by the ice, the ice melts or changes state, but the temperature of the liquid is also 32° F. The heat added during the process of melting the ice at 32° to water at 32° F (at sea level barometric pressure) is the hidden or latent heat of fusion.

This process also works in the reverse order. When water is chilled to 32° F and more heat is taken away to form it into ice at 32° F, this heat is also latent heat of fusion.

Here is where one of the most important laws in physics is involved in refrigeration; heat can never be destroyed. It can only be transferred from one substance to another. So, the same amount of heat required to melt the ice into water must be removed from the water to convert it back to ice.

The latent heat of fusion for pure water at 32° F and at sea-level barometric pressure is 143.33 Btu per pound.

C7. Latent Heat of Vaporization.—As the last of the ice melts, the temperature of the water begins to rise. The temperature causing the rise is sensible heat. When the temperature of water reaches 212° F, the temperature stops rising and another change takes place. More heat is added and the water boils or changes to steam, but there is no change in temperature. This too is hidden heat. As the last of the water vaporizes and more heat is added, the temperature will again rise and again we are dealing with sensible heat.

The heat added to, or taken away, in the process of changing water to steam vapor, or from vapor/steam back to water, is called latent heat of vaporization. All substances that change from liquid to a vapor or gas go through this stage.

The value set for one pound of water at 212° F to be converted into steam, or steam converted to water, is 970.4 Btu. Other changes of state with variation of temperature, and the number of Btu required by such changes for a pound of water, are shown in figure 2.

THEORY OF HEAT

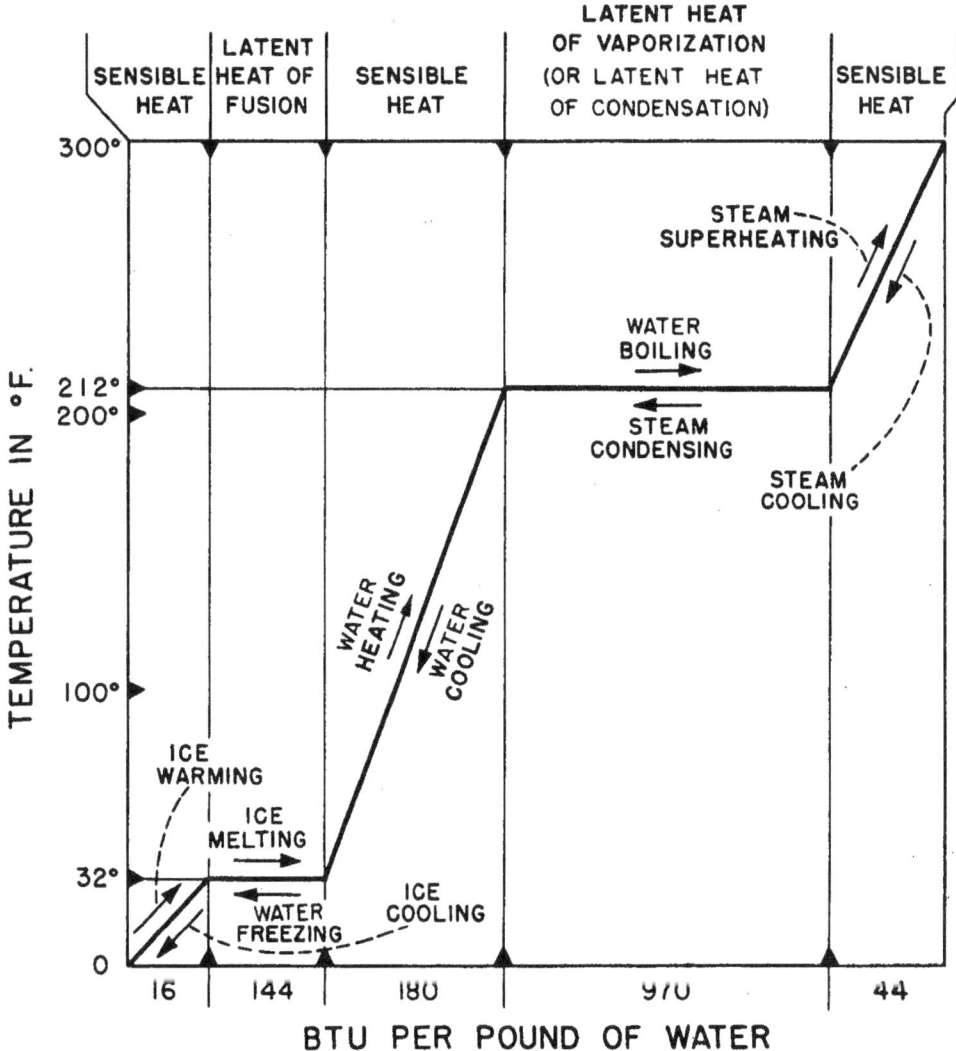

Figure 2.—Relationship between sensible heat and latent heat for water at atmospheric pressure.

C8. Total Heat.—The term total heat is used with two different meanings and care must be used in reading textbooks in order that the meaning intended is properly understood. These two usages are as follows:

Strictly speaking, the total heat of a substance is the total heat energy calculated from absolute zero in Btu. It is specific heat x mass x absolute temperature. Since there is no instrument, however, for measuring heat directly on the absolute scale, and since it would also require high numbers, other starting points are arbitrarily chosen. For the liquid water, the arbitrary starting point is 32° F.

In refrigeration and air conditioning, the total heat of a substance or of the air in a room is all the heat present, that is:

Total Heat = Sensible Heat + Latent Heat

In discussions, the term heat content is sometimes used. This term has the same meaning as total heat.

D. PRESSURE

D1. Atmospheric Pressure.—At the beginning of this chapter, we defined matter as ything which occupies space and has weight. s air is matter, it too has weight. The weight this air is called atmospheric pressure. The lued scale for a column of air 1 inch square cross-sectional area at the base and reaching om sea level to the upper limit of the earth's mosphere at 32° F and at sea level is 14.696 unds. This will vary due to condition changes the air above the earth. For all practical rposes, the value is considered to be 14.7 unds per square inch (psi) at sea level.

D2. Mercury Barometer.—To measure atospheric pressure, scientists have developed simple instrument called a mercury baroeter. It is constructed with a glass tube that a little over thirty inches long and sealed at e end. The tube is then completely filled with ercury. By placing a finger over the open end d inverting into an open dish of mercury, e mercury column in the tube will fall, leavg a vacuum in the space above the mercury. ae air pressure exerted on the surface of the ercury in the dish will maintain a column mercury in the tube equal to the pressure the surface. At sea level pressure of 14.7 i, the height of the column of mercury in e tube will be 29.921 inches. As atmospheric essure is increased or decreased, the height the mercury column will vary in relation to e pressure.

D3. Aneroid Barometer.—Another device ed to measure atmospheric pressure is the eroid barometer. This type is more compact d easier to handle than the mercury baroeter, but not as accurate.

The aneroid barometer consists of an airht metal box, with a partial vacuum inside, d a flexible side that can move slightly under rying pressures. The motion of the flexible de is transmitted through gears and levers a pointer that is calibrated to a scale on the al. This scale is graduated in inches and rresponds to the inches of mercury in the ercury barometer.

A good aneroid barometer will show a slight crease in pressure when lowered from a table the floor.

D4. Conversion of Barometer Readings.— ice the aneroid and mercury barometers incate the atmospheric pressure in inches, a nversion factor must be used to convert this essure to pounds per square inch. At an air temperature of 32° F and at mean sea level, the mercury column stands at 29.921 inches and corresponds to a pressure of 14.696 psi. By dividing 14.696 by 29.921, the result will give the conversion factor of 0.491. To convert the reading on the barometer, multiply the reading by the conversion factor.

D5. Variation of Pressure and Boiling Point with Altitude.—The pressures and boiling points of substances will vary with altitudes. If an uncovered container filled with fresh water at mean sea level is heated until the water boils, a thermometer inserted in the water shows that its temperature is 212° F, and a barometer shows that the atmospheric pressure is approximately 14.7 psi. However, if the pot of boiling water is on a hilltop 1000 feet above sea level, the thermometer shows that the water boils at 210° F when the barometer reads approximately 14.14 psi. Similar variations in boiling point and barometric pressure are observed at different altitudes, as indicated in the following table:

Feet above sea level	Pressure (psi)	Boiling point of Water (°F)
Sea level	14.70	212
2000	13.57	208
4000	12.49	204
6000	11.54	200
8000	10.62	196

D6. Pressure-Temperature Relationship for Change of State.—It is not variations of pressure and temperatures at different altitudes to which special attention is directed, but the relationship between the temperature of vaporization and the corresponding pressure. It is not necessary, however, to go to different heights to obtain different pressures; different pressures may be obtained by mechanical means at any location.

For example, a boiling liquid and its vapor may be contained in an airtight metal cylinder with a piston. By moving the piston in or out, the pressure within may be increased or decreased. If the piston is pushed in, thus increasing the pressure inside, a thermometer shows that the change of state from liquid to vapor requires a temperature higher than 212° F. If the piston is pulled out, thus decreasing the pressure within, the thermometer shows that the change of state from liquid to vapor takes

THEORY OF HEAT

place at a temperature lower than 212° F. Many types of such mechanical arrangements are in common use.

This relationship of vaporization temperature and pressure, which varies for different substances, follows an exact law, and may be tabulated accurately for each substance.

D7. Pressure Gage.—Pressures within an airtight system of pipes, tanks, and cylinders are usually measured by a Bourdon-tube pressure gage. In this gage there is a small tube, flattened (not round) in cross-section, and curved to about three-quarters of a circle. One end of this curved tube is firmly fixed to the mounting, or case; the other end is free and slightly movable. A delicate lever system which turns a pointer on a circular scale is attached to the free end. The fixed end of this tube is joined by connections to the vapor system, and made part of that system. Increases in vapor pressure tend to straighten the curved tube, thus rotating the pointer. The scale is marked to indicate the pressure values in units of pounds per square inch.

The scale on the Bourdon-tube pressure gage is marked with zero to correspond to standard atmospheric pressure. Consequently, zero gage pressure equals 14.7 pounds per square inch. When the pressure of the vapor inside the curved tube is 14.7 psi, it is equal to the atmospheric pressure outside the tube, and there is no tendency for the curved tube to straighten. Hence, this pressure is taken as the zero point on the gage.

'D8. Gage Pressure.—The pressure indicated by a Bourdon-tube pressure gage is in reality the difference between the vapor pressure inside and the air pressure outside the curved tube. Readings from such a gage are always designated gage pressure.

Gage pressure is expressed in pounds per square inch. For convenience, this term is indicated by its abbreviated form psi. Often, where the meaning is unmistakable, the word pounds alone is used; for example, 20 pounds' pressure means 20 pounds per square inch pressure.

D9. Absolute Pressure.—The term absolute pressure is used to designate the true total pressure inside the enclosed vapor system. Suppose the pressure gage stands at 6 pounds. Then, since zero gage pressure means 14.7 pounds inside (to balance 14.7 pounds air pressure outside the tube), the total, or absolute pressure of the vapor is 14.7 pounds plus 6 pounds, or 20.7 pounds. If an accurate knowledge of the pressure is required, the atmospheric pressure, converted from a barometer reading, is used instead of the 14.7-pound standard.

D10. Vacuum or Negative Gage Pressure.—As stated, the standard atmospheric pressure of 14.7 psi is taken as the zero point on the gage. A gage dealing only with increases in pressure has a single scale marked from 0 to 300 pounds, or some other upper limit, and is read in psi gage pressure.

But, pressures may decrease below atmospheric pressure as well as increase. Pressures below 14.7 psi are known as partial vacuums. This term is merely for convenience in referring to pressures below ordinary atmospheric pressure, since such a pressure is far from approaching a vacuum.

A gage that registers pressures lower than standard atmospheric pressure is called a vacuum gage. Such gages are graduated to read in inches of vacuum. Approximately 30 inches of vacuum equal zero pounds absolute pressure.

D11. Compound Gage.—A compound gage is sometimes called a compound pressure and vacuum gage. It has an extended range covering pressures both below and above atmospheric pressure. The scale is graduated to the left and right of zero (atmospheric pressure). Above atmospheric pressure readings are in psi, and below atmospheric pressures are readings of inches of vacuum.

Gages used on the suction side of most refrigeration units are of the compound type.

E. VAPORIZATION

E1. Kinds of Vaporization.—Ebullition, evaporation, and sublimation are the three kinds of vaporization, or methods of converting from one physical state to another.

E2. Ebullition.—Ebullition is the technical term for ordinary boiling. It is a rapid and visible process. By looking into an uncovered container of boiling water, one can see that ebullition, or boiling, is taking place. Starting from the bottom and sides, large and small bubbles rise to the surface and escape from the liquid.

E3. **Evaporation.**—Evaporation is a slow and invisible process which takes place only from the surface of a liquid. Under ordinary conditions, evaporation cannot be seen. Any liquid in an uncovered container will gradually evaporate, its level slowly falling until all liquid is gone. Water continually evaporates from the surface of all open bodies such as rivers, lakes, ponds, and oceans. Wet clothing, hung on a line to dry, does so, by this process.

Since evaporation is a form of vaporization, it results in the removal of latent heat. Therefore, it is a cooling process, though a slow one. When a person goes in swimming on a cool day with a wind blowing, it is the evaporation process that makes him feel uncomfortable, rather than the temperature itself. The human body gets rid of excess heat and moisture naturally and continually by evaporation.

Some liquids evaporate much faster than others. For example, alcohol will evaporate much faster than water.

E4. **Sublimation.**—The third method of converting from one physical state to another is called sublimation. It consists of converting from a solid directly to the vapor state without passing through the intermediate or liquid state. Ice and snow, even when much below the freezing point, slowly disappear without melting. Washed clothes, hung out-of-doors in temperatures below 32° F, first freeze stiff, and then dry soft. Both these phenomena are caused by sublimation.

Sublimation has little application to refrigeration engineering. It has, however, considerable use in the small scale cooling of bottled foods, ice cream, and other food stuffs by the use of solid carbon dioxide, or dry ice, which sublimes to a vapor under atmospheric pressure.

E5. **Vapor and Gas.**—The terms vapor and gas both refer to matter in the physical state that is neither solid or liquid. There is, however, a definite distinction between the two.

Vapor condenses very readily to a liquid state under small changes of temperature or pressure, or both, and constantly does so under ordinary conditions of nature. It may be said to be very close to the liquid state, although it is a vapor.

Gas, on the other hand, exists under ordinary conditions in a gaseous state. To change it to a liquid state, special laboratory apparatus capable of producing extreme changes of pressure is required. A gas may be said to be far removed from the liquid state and cannot change under ordinary natural conditions.

In refrigeration, the word gas is frequently used instead of the more correct term vapor.

F. PHYSICIAL CONDITIONS OF VAPORS AND LIQUIDS

F1. **State and Condition.**—The term state is used to refer to the three forms of matter: solid, liquid, and gas or vapor. However, a substance in any one of the three states may be found in different conditions. Hence, the term condition is also used. A vapor ordinarily exists in either of two conditions, as a saturated vapor or as superheated vapor.

F2. **Saturated Vapor.**—The saturated vapor is a vapor at the temperature corresponding to its boiling point at a given pressure. Saturated vapors are classed as either wet or dry. If they contain liquid particles of their substance, they are termed wet. If no particles are present, they are termed dry.

Saturated vapors are usually in the wet state due to the boiling action of the substance. The bubbles, as they break away from the surface as a vapor, will carry tiny droplets of the liquid suspended in the vapor.

F3. **Superheated Vapor.**—If a vapor is not in contact with a boiling liquid, either because the liquid has been converted into vapor or because the vapor has been separated from the boiling liquid, further application of heat produces a rise in temperature of the vapor under the same given pressure. Such a vapor is called superheated vapor.

F4. **Saturation Temperature.**—If a liquid is heated, it finally boils at a temperature that is the result of the pressure present. Such a temperature is called the saturation temperature corresponding to the given pressure. This term is frequently used in air conditioning and means the boiling point, or the condensation point, at the given pressure.

A liquid that is at the saturation temperature corresponding to a given pressure, and is under that pressure, is called a saturated liquid.

G. EXPANSION AND CONTRACTION OF SUBSTANCE

G.1. **General.**—In general, all substances, whether solid, liquid, or gas, decrease in volume when cooled and increase in volume when heated. In gases and vapors, the amount of change is large; in liquids and solids it is small. In all cases, great forces are produced and it is necessary in all engineering construction to allow for the operation of these forces. Different substances vary in the amount of change in volume they undergo for the same differences in temperature.

G2. **Expansion and Contraction of Water.**—Water contracts as it is cooled until the temperature 39.2°F is reached. At this point the change in volume reverses and if the water is cooled further, the volume increases. When water freezes into ice, an enormous force is brought into play. This force is sufficient to split large rocks, burst iron pipes and even steel tanks, unless provisions are allowed for the expansion.

G3. **Expansion and Contraction at the Change of State.**—At their melting point, substances follow no general rule regarding expansion and contraction. Some metals like iron, bismuth, and antimony, contract on melting and expand on solidifying; but most others like gold, silver, and copper, expand on melting and contract on solidifying. All liquids, however, expand greatly when changing into a vapor unless constrained mechanically, as in a closed container. An example of this expansion is the large clouds of steam continually rising from a container of boiling water.

G4. **Specific Volume.**—The specific volume of a substance is a number that indicates the number of cubic feet occupied by one pound of the substance at a given temperature and pressure. Specific volume varies greatly for different substances and for the same substances at different temperatures and pressures.

The specific volume for boiling water at atmospheric pressure is 0.0167 cubic feet per pound, and of steam at the same pressure it is 26.79 cubic feet per pound. Thus, water in changing its state from liquid to vapor at ordinary atmospheric pressure increases in volume 1604 times.

H. HEAT TRANSFER

H1. **How Heat is Transferred.**—As explained earlier in this chapter, heat can neither be created nor destroyed, but only transferred from one substance to another. This transfer is accomplished through one of three ways: radiation, convection, and conduction.

H2. **Radiation.**—In radiation, heat is transmitted through empty space (a vacuum), as from the sun to the earth's atmosphere. Heat, light, electricity, radio, and x-rays are all known to be energy in the form of transverse vibrations. Physically, they differ only in their wave lengths, but their physical effects are quite different, as is evident by comparing heat with radio waves. In radiation, nothing but energy really travels.

Radiation does not heat the air through which it passes, it heats only the objects on which it falls. Not only the sun, but other objects such as flames, stoves, electric light bulbs, machines, and the earth itself, radiate heat. Even our bodies radiate heat.

H3. **Convection.**—Convection is the transfer of heat by the movement of a substance (gas or liquid) through a space. Examples of this include a current of warm air in a room, a current of warm water such as the Gulf Stream, and warm air rising from a hot water or steam radiator.

H4. **Conduction.**—The transfer of heat from one molecule to another, either of the same substance or of different substances, by direct contact is called conduction. A molecule of a substance is the smallest particle of a substance that retains the special qualities of that substance. Any further subdivision of a molecule separates it into the atoms of which it is composed.

Physical contact is necessary for conduction of heat, and the conduction takes place from the region of the higher temperature to the lower temperature. For example, if a person holds a metal bar of iron in one hand and places the other end of the bar in a fire, the heat passes from the fire to the bar, then along the bar to the hand. Here physical contact is made in each instance; fire to bar, bar to hand.

H5. **Thermal Conductance.**—Suppose that two bars are held, one of iron and one of copper, of exactly the same size and at the same temperature. If one end of each bar is placed in a fire at the same time, heat will reach the hand holding the copper bar more quickly than through the iron bar. This is cause some substances conduct heat more readily than others.

This characteristic of a substance is called its thermal or heat conductance. The low and high thermal conductance of substances is of great importance in refrigeration and air conditioning. Some substances are used for transfer of heat while others are used to prevent heat transfer.

I. INSULATION

I1. **Need for Insulation.**—It is comparatively easy to heat or cool articles or enclosed spaces. It is not easy, however, to keep them at a constant temperature because heat constantly tends to flow to the lower temperature areas.

When it is desired to keep a space within a certain temperature range, it is necessary to prevent the transfer of heat to or from the space. Fortunately this can be done, fairly successfully, by the use of a substance with low thermal conductance.

I2. **Insulators.**—Poor conductors are good insulators. Poor conductors include such substances as cork, wood, sawdust, paper, brick, rubber, fur, feathers, felt, plastics, cotton, and dead air space. Most solids that are poor conductors are also porous in nature, and the pores or air cells are small in size. Much of the insulating quality results from these tiny pockets.

The "K" conductivity factor for an insulating material is the amount of Btu per square foot, per hour, per °F, that can penetrate the insulation for a thickness of one inch. Some of the more commonly used insulating materials and "K" conductivity factors follow:

Material	"K" Factor
Cork with pitch	0.428
Sawdust, pine	0.57
Wool, pure	0.26
Glass	5.0
Air (dead)	0.175

I3. **Low Temperature Insulation.**—The requirements for low-temperature insulation are somewhat different from those for high-temperature insulation. Any water vapor present in the air tends to condense into liquid droplets or film on a cold surface. This is commonly called sweating. This condensed water penetrates a porous material and fills the air cells, lessening its insulating ability. It may freeze there and ice is a very poor insulator of heat. Insulating materials for use with refrigeration systems are manufactured to resist the penetration of moisture, and to be durable under conditions of high humidity.

Low-temperature pipe lines must be thoroughly insulated to prevent heat from entering the refrigerant contained therein. The usual insulation is a cork composition molded into sections that fit snugly around the pipes and fittings. Other materials, such as rock wool and mineral wool, are also used in the same way.

Before applying the covering, all pipes should be carefully cleaned, all rust removed, and dried. If possible, the hangers and braces should be attached around the outside of the insulation to prevent the transfer of heat by conduction and to prevent moisture from entering the insulation.

When molded sections are installed on pipe lines, they should be staggered and all joints should be placed so as to come together at the top and bottom of the pipe. After all seams are sealed, the covering should be painted with an asphalt paint, to make it waterproof.

Always repair ruptured insulation as soon as possible to prevent the entry of moisture. Make sure the pipe is dry and all seams are sealed when making repairs.

REFRIGERATION AND AIR CONDITIONING TERMINOLOGY AND TROUBLESHOOTING

TABLE OF CONTENTS

 |Page
---|---

A. TERMINOLOGY

	Page
Absolute Pressure ... Bimetallic Element	1
Boiling Point ... Conduction	2
Conductor (Heat or Thermal) ... Equalizer	3
Evaporation ... Humidistat	4
Humidity ... Saturated Liquid	5
Saturated Vapor ... Wet-Bulb Depression	6

B. TROUBLESHOOTING   7

REFRIGERATION AND AIR CONDITIONING

TERMINOLOGY AND TROUBLESHOOTING

A. TERMINOLOGY

Many of the terms used in connection with refrigeration and air conditioning have quite definite and specialized meanings. In order to understand any written material in the field of refrigeration and air conditioning, it is essential to have a thorough knowledge of correct terminology. Some important terms used in connection with refrigeration and air conditioning are defined in the following list.

ABSOLUTE PRESSURE.—Pressure measured from absolute zero rather than from normal atmospheric pressure; the sum of atmospheric pressure plus gage pressure.

ABSOLUTE TEMPERATURE.—Temperature measured from absolute zero (-459.67° F, or -273.15°C).

ABSORBENT.—A material that has the ability to extract certain substances from a liquid or a gas with which it is in contact, causing physical changes, chemical changes, or both during the absorption process.

ACCUMULATOR.—A shell placed in a suction line for separating liquid refrigerant entrained in suction gas; serves as a storage chamber for low side liquid refrigerant; also known as a surge drum or surge header.

ADIABATIC PROCESS.—Any thermodynamic process that is accomplished without the transfer of heat to or from the system while the process is occurring.

ADSORBENT.—A material that has the ability to cause molecules of gases, liquids, and solids to adhere to its internal surfaces without causing any chemical or physical change.

AIR CONDITIONING.—The process of treating air to simultaneously control its temperature, humidity, cleanliness, and distribution to meet the requirements of the conditioned space.

AIR CONDITIONING UNIT.—An assembly of equipment for the control of (at least) the temperature, humidity, and cleanliness of the air within a conditioned space.

AIR DIFFUSER.—A device arranged to promote the mixing of the air leaving the duct with the room air.

AMBIENT AIR TEMPERATURE.—The temperature of the air surrounding an object; in a system using an air-cooled condenser, the temperature of the air entering the condenser.

ANEMOMETER.—An instrument for measuring the velocity of air flow.

ATMOSPHERIC PRESSURE.—Pressure exerted by the weight of the atmosphere; standard atmospheric pressure is 14.696 psia or 29.921 inches of mercury at sea level.

BACK PRESSURE.—Same as suction pressure.

BAFFLE.—A partition to direct the flow of a fluid.

BAROMETER.—An instrument for measuring atmospheric pressure.

BAROMETRIC PRESSURE.—The actual atmospheric pressure existing at any given moment; at certain times, barometric pressure is not identical with standard atmospheric pressure.

BIMETALLIC ELEMENT.—A device formed from two different metals having different

TERMINOLOGY AND TROUBLESHOOTING

coefficients of thermal expansion; used in temperature indicating and controlling instruments.

BOILING POINT.—Temperature at which a liquid boils at a given pressure.

BORE.—Inside diameter of a cylinder.

BRINE.—Any liquid cooled by the refrigerant and used for the transmission of heat without change of state.

BRITISH THERMAL UNIT.—The amount of heat required to produce a temperature rise of 1° F in 1 pound of water. Abbreviated Btu.

CENTIGRADE.—A thermometric system in which the freezing point of water is 0° C and the boiling point of water is 100° C, at standard atmospheric pressure.

CENTRAL FAN SYSTEM.—A mechanical, indirect system of air conditioning in which the air is treated by equipment outside the area served and is conveyed to and from the area by means of a fan and a distributing duct system.

CENTRIFUGAL MACHINE.—A compressor employing centrifugal force for compression.

CHANGE OF AIR.—The introduction of new, cleansed, or recirculated air to conditioned spaces, measured in the number of complete air changes in a specified time.

CHANGE OF STATE.—The change from one phase (solid, liquid, or gas) to another.

CHARGE.—The amount of refrigerant in a system; also the act of putting refrigerant into a system.

CHILL.—To refrigerate meats, water, etc., moderately, without freezing.

COEFFICIENT OF EXPANSION.—The change in length per unit length per degree of change in temperature of a material; or the change in volume per unit volume per degree of change in temperature of a material.

COEFFICIENT OF PERFORMANCE.—The ratio of the refrigeration produced to the work supplied, with refrigeration and work being expressed in the same units.

COIL.—Any cooling or heating element made of pipe or tubing.

COMFORT CHART.—A chart showing effective temperature, with dry-bulb temperature and humidity, by which the effects of various conditions on human comfort may be determined.

COMFORT COOLING.—Refrigeration for comfort, as opposed to refrigeration for manufacture or storage.

COMFORT ZONE.—The range of effective temperatures over which the majority of adults feel comfortable.

COMPRESSION, MULTI-STAGE. — Compression in two or more stages, as when the discharge of one compressor is connected to the suction of another.

COMPRESOR, HERMETIC.—A compressor in which the electric motor and the compressor are enclosed within a sealed housing.

COMPRESSOR, "V" AND "W".—High speed, single-acting, multi-cylinder compressor with straight-line piston movement in the various cylinders; the cylinders are in the "V" position or the "W" position with respect to the shaft axis.

CONDENSATE.—The liquid formed by the condensation of a vapor. In steam heating, water condensed from steam; in air conditioning, water removed from air by condensation on the cooling coil of a refrigeration system.

CONDENSATION.—The process by which a vapor changes to a liquid when heat is removed from the vapor.

CONDENSER.—A vessel or an arrangement of pipe or tubing in which the compressed refrigerant vapor is liquefied by the removal of heat.

CONDENSING UNIT.—A specific refrigerating machine combination for a given refrigerant; the unit consists of one or more power-driven compressors, condensers, liquid receivers (when required), and the necessary accessories.

CONDUCTION.—The method of heat transfer by which heat is transferred from molecule to

REFRIGERATION AND AIR CONDITIONING

molecule within a homogeneous substance or between two substances that are in physical contact with each other.

CONDUCTOR (HEAT OR THERMAL).—A material that readily transmits heat by conduction; the opposite of an insulator.

CONTROL.—Any device for the regulation of a machine in normal operation. May be manual or automatic; if automatic, it is responsive to changes in temperature, pressure, liquid level, time, or other variables.

CONVECTION.—The movement of a mass of fluid (liquid or gas) caused by differences in density in different parts of the fluid; the differences in density are caused by differences in temperature. As the fluid moves, it carries with it its contained heat energy, which is then transferred from one part of the fluid to another and from the fluid to the surroundings.

COOLER, OIL.—A heat exchanger used for cooling oil in a lubrication system.

COOLING TOWER.—A device for lowering the temperature of water by evaporative cooling, as the water is showered through a space in which outside air is circulated.

COOLING WATER.—Water used in a condenser to cool and condense a refrigerant.

COPPER PLATING.—The depositing of a film of copper on the surface of another metal (such as iron or steel) by electrochemical action; in refrigeration, copper plating usually occurs on compressor walls, pistons, discharge valves, shafts, and seals.

COUNTERFLOW.—In a heat exchanger, opposite direction of flow of the cooling liquid and the cooled liquid (or of the heating liquid and the heated liquid).

CRYOGENICS.—The branch of physics that relates to the production and the effects of very low temperatures.

CYCLE.—The complete course of operation of a refrigerant, from starting point back to starting point, in a closed refrigeration system; also, a general term for any repeated process in any system.

DEGREE.—Unit of temperature.

DEGREE OF SUPERHEAT.—The amount by which the temperature of a superheated vapor exceeds the temperature of the saturated vapor at the same pressure.

DEHUMIDIFIER.—An air cooler or washer used for lowering the moisture content of the air passing through it.

DEHUMIDIFY.—To reduce, by any process, the quantity of water vapor within a given space.

DEHYDRATE.—To remove water (in any form) from some other substance.

DENSITY.—Mass per unit volume or weight per unit volume.

DESICCANT.—Any absorbent or adsorbent, liquid or solid, that removes water or water vapor from a material. In a refrigeration circuit, the desiccant should be insoluble in the refrigerant and refrigerant oils.

DEWPOINT.—The temperature at which water vapor begins to condense in any given sample of air; dewpoint depends upon humidity, temperature, and pressure.

DISTRIBUTOR.—A device for guiding the flow of liquid into parallel paths in an evaporator.

DRIER.—A device containing a desiccant placed in a refrigerant circuit for the purpose of collecting and holding within the desiccant all water in the system above the amount that can be tolerated in the circulating refrigerant.

ELECTROLYSIS.—Chemical decomposition caused by action of an electric current in a solution.

ENTHALPY.—A term used to mean TOTAL HEAT or HEAT CONTENT.

EQUALIZER.—Piping arrangement on an enclosed compressor to equalize refrigerant gas pressure in the crankcase and suction; device for dividing the liquid refrigerant between parallel low-side coils; a piping arrangement to divide the lubricating oil between the crankcases of compressors operating in parallel; the method by which refrigerant pressure is

TERMINOLOGY AND TROUBLESHOOTING

transmitted to the diaphragm or bellows of a thermostatic expansion valve.

EVAPORATION.—The change of state from the liquid phase to the vapor phase.

EVAPORATOR.—The unit in a refrigeration system in which the refrigerant is vaporized to produce refrigeration.

EXFILTRATION.—The flow of air outward from a space through walls, leaks, etc.

EXPANSION VALVE SUPERHEAT.—The difference between the temperature of the thermal bulb and the temperature corresponding to the pressure at the coil outlet or at the equalizer connection (where provided).

FAHRENHEIT.—Thermometric scale in which 32° F denotes the freezing point of water and 212° F denotes the boiling temperature of water under standard atmospheric pressure at sea level.

FIN.—An extended surface used on tubes in some heat exchangers to increase the heat transfer area.

FLASH CHAMBER. — A separation tank placed between the expansion valve and the evaporator in a refrigeration system to separate and bypass any flash gas formed in the expansion valve.

FLASH GAS.—The gas resulting from the instantaneous evaporation of refrigerant in a pressure-reducing device, to cool the refrigerant to the evaporating temperature corresponding to the reduced pressure.

FLUID.—The general term that includes liquids and gases (or vapors).

FOAMING.—The formation of a foam or froth on an oil-refrigerant mixture; caused by a reduction in pressure with consequent rapid boiling out of the refrigerant.

FREEZING.—The change of state from the liquid phase to the solid phase.

GAGE PRESSURE.—Absolute pressure minus atmospheric pressure.

GAS.—A substance in the gaseous state; a highly superheated vapor that satisfies the perfect gas laws, within acceptable limits of accuracy. See VAPOR.

GAS, INERT.—A gas that does not readily enter into or cause chemical reactions.

GAS, NONCONDENSABLE.—A gas in a refrigeration system which does not condense at the temperature and partial pressure existing in the condenser, thereby exerting a higher head pressure on the system.

GRILLE.—A lattice or grating for an intake opening or a delivery opening.

HEAD PRESSURE.—The operating pressure measured in the discharge line at the compressor outlet.

HEAT.—A basic form of energy, which is transferred by virtue of a temperature difference.

HEAT OF CONDENSATION.—The latent heat given up by a substance as it changes from a gas to a liquid.

HEAT OF FUSION.—The latent heat absorbed when a substance changes from a solid state to a liquid state.

HEAT OF VAPORIZATION.—The latent heat absorbed by a substance as it changes from a liquid to a vapor.

HEAT PUMP.—Refrigeration equipment; used for year-round air conditioning. In summer used to cool and condition the air in a space; in winter used to warm and condition the air.

HOT-GAS DEFROSTING.—The use of high pressure or condenser gas in the low side or condenser gas in the evaporator to effect the removal of frost.

HUMIDIFY.—To increase the percentage of water vapor within a given space.

HUMIDISTAT.—A control instrument or device, actuated by changes in humidity within the conditioned areas, which automatically regulates the relative humidity of the area.

REFRIGERATION AND AIR CONDITIONING

HUMIDITY.—The water vapor within a given space.

HUMIDITY, SPECIFIC.—The weight of water vapor mixed with 1 pound of dry air, expressed as the number of grains of moisture per pound of dry air.

HYDROLYSIS.—The splitting up of compounds by reaction with water. For example, the reaction of R-12 with water which results in the formation of acid materials.

INDUSTRIAL AIR CONDITIONING.—Air conditioning used for purposes other than comfort.

JACKET WATER.—The water used to cool the cylinder head and cylinder walls of a water-cooled compressor.

LATENT HEAT.—Heat transfer that is NOT reflected in a temperature change but IS reflected in a changing physical state of the substance involved.

LIQUEFACTION.—The change of state from a gas to a liquid. (The term liquefaction is usually used instead of condensation when referring to substances which are in a gaseous state at ordinary pressures and temperatures.)

LIQUID LINE.—The tube or pipe through which liquid refrigerant is carried from the condenser or receiver to the pressure-reducing device.

LIQUID RECEIVER.—A vessel permanently connected to the high side of a system for the storage of liquefied refrigerant.

LOAD.—The amount of heat imposed upon a refrigeration system in any specified period of time, or the required rate of heat removal; usually expressed in Btu per hour.

LOW SIDE.—The parts of the refrigeration system that are at or below the evaporating temperature.

MANOMETER.—A U-tube, or a single tube and reservoir arrangement, used with a suitable fluid to measure pressure differences.

MELTING.—The change of state from a solid to a liquid.

OZONE.—Triatomic oxygen (O_3). Sometimes used in cold storage or air conditioning installations as an odor eliminator. Can be toxic in certain concentrations.

PLENUM CHAMBER.—An air compartment maintained under pressure for receiving air before distribution to the conditioned spaces.

PNEUMATIC.—Operated by air pressure.

PREHEATING.—In air conditioning, to heat the air in advance of other processes.

PRESSURE.—Force per unit area.

PRESSURE DROP.—Loss of pressure, as from one end of a refrigerant line to the other, because of friction.

PRESSURE EQUALIZING.—Allowing the high side and the low side of the refrigeration system to become equal or nearly equal in pressure during idle periods, to prevent excessive starting loads on the compressor.

PRESSURE REGULATOR, SUCTION.—An automatic valve designed to limit the suction pressure to prevent motor overload.

PSYCHROMETER.—An instrument for measuring relative humidities by means of wet-bulb and dry-bulb temperatures.

PSYCHROMETRIC CHART.—A graphical representation of the properties of water vapor and air mixtures.

PURGING.—The act of blowing out gas from a refrigeration system, usually for the purpose of removing air or other noncondensable gases.

REFRIGERATION TON.—The removal of heat at a rate of 288,000 Btu in 24 hours or 12,000 Btu in 1 hour.

RETURN AIR.—The air returned from a space being conditioned.

SATURATED LIQUID.—A liquid which is at saturation pressure and saturation temperature; in other words, a liquid which is at its boiling point for any given pressure.

TERMINOLOGY AND TROUBLESHOOTING

SATURATED VAPOR.—A vapor which is at saturation pressure and saturation temperature. A saturated vapor cannot be superheated as long as it is in contact with the liquid from which it is being generated.

SATURATION PRESSURE and SATURATION TEMPERATURE.—The pressure and temperature at which a liquid and the vapor it is generating can exist in equilibrium contact with each other. The boiling point of any liquid depends upon pressure and temperature; a liquid boils when it is at the saturation temperature for any particular saturation pressure.

SELF-CONTAINED UNIT.—A refrigeration unit that can be removed from the premises without disconnecting any refrigerant-containing part.

SENSIBLE HEAT.—Heat transfer that is reflected in a change of temperature.

SILICA GEL.—A form of silicon dioxide which absorbs moisture readily; used as a drying agent.

SPECIFIC GRAVITY.—The density of a substance compared to the density of a standard material such as water.

SPECIFIC VOLUME.—The space occupied by unit amount of a substance at a specified pressure and temperature; often measured in cubic feet per pound.

SUBCOOLED LIQUID.—A liquid that is at a temperature below its boiling point for any given pressure.

SUBCOOLING.—The process of cooling a liquid to a temperature below its saturation temperature for any given saturation pressure.

SUPERHEATING.—The process of adding heat to a vapor in order to raise its temperature above saturation temperature. It is impossible to superheat a saturated vapor as long as it is in contact with the liquid from which it is being generated; hence the vapor must be led away from the liquid before it can be superheated.

TEMPERATURE.—A measure of the concentration of heat (thermal energy) in a body or substance.

THERMODYNAMICS.—The branch of physics that deals with heat and its transformations to and from other forms of energy.

THERMOSTAT.—A temperature-sensing automatic control device.

TOXIC.—Having temporary or permanent poisonous effects.

TUBE, CAPILLARY.—In refrigeration, a tube of small internal diameter used as a liquid refrigerant flow control or expansion device between the high side and the low side of the refrigeration system.

UNLOADER.—A device in or on the compressor for equalizing high-side and low-side pressures for a brief time during starting and for controlling compressor capacity by rendering one or more cylinders ineffective.

VACUUM.—Pressure that is less than atmospheric pressure.

VALVE, KING.—A stop valve between the receiver and the expansion valve, normally close to the receiver.

VAPOR.—A gaseous substance, particularly one that is at or near saturation temperature and pressure.

VENTILATION.—The process of supplying or removing air by natural or mechanical means, to or from a space; such air may or may not have been conditioned.

VITAL HEAT.—The heat generated by fruits and vegetables in storage; caused by ripening.

VOLATILE LIQUID.—A liquid that evaporates (vaporizes) readily at atmospheric pressure and room temperature.

WATER (OR BRINE) COOLER.—A factory-made assembly or elements in which the water or brine and the refrigerant are in heat transfer relationship causing the refrigerant to evaporate and absorb heat from the water or brine.

WATER VAPOR.—In air conditioning, the water in the atmosphere.

WET-BULB DEPRESSION.—The difference between the dry-bulb temperature and the wet-bulb temperature.

REFRIGERATION AND AIR CONDITIONING

B. TROUBLESHOOTING

The two trouble charts that follow may be used as a guide for locating and correcting malfunctions in refrigeration systems. The first chart deals with troubles that may be encountered in vapor compression systems. The second chart deals with troubles that may be encountered in absorption-type (lithium bromide) systems. If the points and procedures outlined in these charts are closely adhered to, a great deal of time can be saved in troubleshooting.

To use these charts, the first thing to do is to isolate the trouble. Then check all possible causes. And finally, make the indicated corrections. In general, the correction of a malfunction is a process of elimination. The easiest corrections should be made first; then, if necessary, the more difficult corrections should be made.

TERMINOLOGY AND TROUBLESHOOTING

Trouble	Possible Cause	Corrective Measure
High condensing pressure.	Air on non-condensable gas in system.	Purge air from condenser.
	Inlet water warm.	Increase quantity of condensing water.
	Insufficient water flowing through condenser.	Increase quantity of water.
	Condenser tubes clogged or scaled.	Clean condenser water tubes.
	Too much liquid in receiver, condenser tubes submerged in liquid refrigerant.	Draw off liquid into service cylinder.
Low condensing pressure.	Too much water flowing through condenser.	Reduce quantity of water.
	Water too cold.	Reduce quantity of water.
	Liquid refrigerant flooding back from evaporator.	Change expansion valve adjustment, examine fastening of thermal bulb.
	Leaky discharge valve.	Remove head, examine valves. Replace any found defective.
High suction pressure.	Overfeeding of expansion valve.	Regulate expansion valve, check bulb attachment.
	Leaky suction valve.	Remove head, examine valve and replace if worn.
Low suction pressure.	Restricted liquid line and expansion valve or suction screens.	Pump down, remove, examine and clean screens.
	Insufficient refrigerant in system.	Check for refrigerant storage.
	Too much oil circulating in system.	Check for too much oil in circulation. Remove oil.
	Improper adjustment of expansion valves.	Adjust valve to give more flow.
	Expansion valve power element dead or weak.	Replace expansion valve power element.

Trouble Chart for Vapor Compression Refrigeration Systems.

REFRIGERATION AND AIR CONDITIONING

Trouble	Possible Cause	Corrective Measure
Compressor short cycles on low pressure control.	Low refrigerant charge.	Locate and repair leaks. Charge refrigerant.
	Thermal expansion valve not feeding properly. (a) Dirty strainers. (b) Moisture frozen in orifice or orifice plugged with dirt. (c) Power element dead or weak.	Adjust, repair or replace thermal expansion valve. (a) Clean strainers. (b) Remove moisture or dirt (Use system dehydrator). (c) Replace power element.
	Water flow through evaporators restricted or stopped. Evaporator coils plugged, dirty, or clogged with frost.	Remove restriction. Check water flow. Clean coils or tubes.
	Defective low pressure control switch.	Repair or replace low pressure control switch.
Compressor runs continuously.	Shortage of refrigerant.	Repair leak and recharge system.
	Leaking discharge valves.	Replace discharge valves.
Compressor short cycles on high pressure control switch.	Insufficient water flowing through condenser, clogged condenser.	Determine if water has been turned off. Check for scaled or fouled condenser.
	Defective high pressure control switch.	Repair or replace high pressure control switch.
Compressor will not run.	Seized compressor.	Repair or replace compressor.
	Cut-in point of low pressure control switch too high.	Set L.P. control switch to cut-in at correct pressure.
	High pressure control switch does not cut-in. 1. Defective switch. 2. Electric power cut off. 3. Service or disconnect switch open.	Check discharge pressure and reset H.P. control switch. 1. Repair or replace switch. 2. Check power supply. 3. Close switches.

Trouble Chart for Vapor Compression Refrigeration Systems—Continued.

TERMINOLOGY AND TROUBLESHOOTING

Trouble	Possible Cause	Corrective Measure
Compressor will not run. (Cont'd)	4. Fuses blown.	4. Test fuses and renew if necessary.
	5. Over-load relays tripped.	5. Re-set relays and find cause of overload.
	6. Low voltage.	6. Check voltage (should be within 10 percent of nameplate rating).
	7. Electrical motor in trouble.	7. Repair or replace motor.
	8. Trouble in starting switch or control circuit.	8. Close switch manually to test power supply. If OK check control circuit including temperature and pressure controls.
	9. Compressor motor stopped by oil pressure differential switch.	9. Check oil level in crankcase. Check oil pump pressure.
Sudden loss of oil from crankcase.	Liquid refrigerant slugging back to compressor crank case.	Adjust or replace expansion valve.
Capacity reduction system fails to unload cylinders.	Hand operating stem of capacity control valve not turned to automatic position.	Set hand operating stem to automatic position.
Compressor continues to operate at full or partial load.	Pressure regulating valve not opening.	Adjust or repair pressure regulating valve.
Capacity reduction system fails to load cylinders.	Broken or leaking oil tube between pump and power element.	Repair leak.
Compressor continues to operate unloaded.	Pressure regulating valve not closing.	Adjust or repair pressure regulating valve.

Trouble Chart for Vapor Compression Refrigeration Systems—Continued.

REFRIGERATION AND AIR CONDITIONING

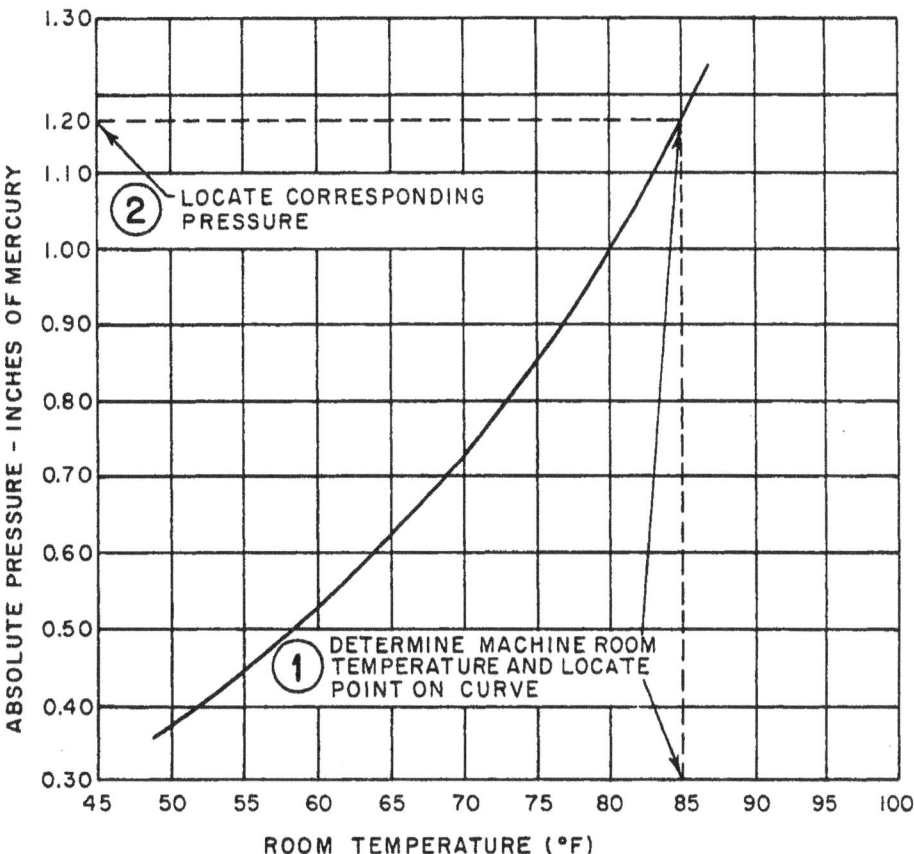

Figure 1.—Pressure temperature curve for lithium-bromide machine.

TROUBLE CHART FOR ABSORPTION TYPE (LITHIUM-BROMIDE) REFRIGERATION SYSTEM

TROUBLE: SOLUTION SOLIDIFIED AT START-UP

	CAUSE	CHECK	CORRECTION
1.	Dilution cycle too short.	- dilution cycle time delay relay.	-Reset time delay relay to 10 minutes.
2.	Steam valve did not close during dilution cycle.	- operation of steam valve and steam EP relay.	-Repair faulty operation. Steam EP relay should close when stop button is pushed and control air pressure at steam valve should go to 0 PSIG.
3.	Cooling load lost during dilution cycle.	- Shut down procedure.	Make certain that the cooling load remains on during the dilution cycle.

TERMINOLOGY AND TROUBLESHOOTING

TROUBLE CHART FOR ABSORPTION TYPE (LITHIUM-BROMIDE) REFRIGERATION SYSTEM—Continued.

TROUBLE: SOLUTION SOLIDIFIED AT START-UP—Continued

	CAUSE	CHECK	CORRECTION
4.	Condenser sea water too cold.	- 3 way mixing valve and sea water thermostat.	-Maintain a constant inlet sea water temperature of 85°F.
5.	Air in machine.	- absolute pressure indicator before starting.	-Turn "Not Purged-Purged" switch to "Not Purged" until machine vacuum corresponds to that given in Fig. 12-1. Find reason for air entering machine.
6.	Machine shut down on safety.	-All safety switches and settings. The following safeties will do this: 1. Low temp. cutout. 2. High temp. cutout. 3. Chilled water pump overload. 4. Absorber - generator pump overload. 5. Refrigerant pump overload. 6. Chilled water failure switch.	-Correct reason for safety cutout or reason for pump overload. -Correct reason for loss of chilled water flow.

TROUBLE: OVER CONCENTRATION OF SOLUTION IN ABSORBER

	CAUSE	CHECK	CORRECTION
1.	High solution temperature in absorber	- solution temperature at generator pump and condensing water temperature leaving absorber. If difference is greater than 10°F, poor heat transfer is indicated.	Add octyl alcohol. If this does not correct the trouble, clean the absorber tubes and check condensing water flow through the absorber.
2.	Plugged spray nozzles in absorber	- discharge pressure of the absorber pump. This should be approximately 11" Hg. Vac.	Inspect and clean spray header and nozzles.

REFRIGERATION AND AIR CONDITIONING

TROUBLE CHART FOR ABSORPTION TYPE (LITHIUM-BROMIDE) REFRIGERATION SYSTEM—Continued.

TROUBLE: OVER CONCENTRATION OF SOLUTION IN ABSORBER—Continued

CAUSE	CHECK	CORRECTION
3. Low condensing sea water flow	- condensing water rise across absorber. At full load this should be 10°F or lower.	Clean inlet sea water strainer. Reset condenser bypass valve.
4. Air in machine	- refrigerant vapor pressure to absorber vapor pressure. Measure temperature at discharge of refrigerant pump and read corresponding vapor pressure on equilibrium diagram. Should be 2° or 3°F.	Reset purge pressure stat to allow more purge operation.
5. Insufficient purging	- purge cycle. With purge pump in operation the purge pump cycle should be about 1 - 1/2 hours. - specific gravity and temperature of purge solution.	Adjust drip tube. Purge valve not opening. This should be about 70° or less with a specific gravity of 1.57 or more to give a purge vapor pressure of less than .18" Hg.
	- pump impeller and jet evacuator for wear	If worn - replace
	- purge system for leaks	Turn off purge pump at the panel board. Blank off the carbon filter tube. Raise pressure in purge system to 25 PSIG and leak test. Correct any leaks

TROUBLE: POOR EVAPORATOR PERFORMANCE

CAUSE	CHECK	CORRECTION
1. Fouled heat transfer surface on chilled water coil	- at full load, check spread between evaporator temperature (at discharge of refrigerant pump) and	Clean tubes - chilled water side. Check division plate gasket in water box, if

TERMINOLOGY AND TROUBLESHOOTING

TROUBLE CHART FOR ABSORPTION TYPE (LITHIUM-BROMIDE) REFRIGERATION SYSTEM—Continued.

TROUBLE: Poor Evaporator Performance—Continued.

CAUSE	CHECK	CORRECTION
	leaving chilled water temperature. Spread should not be greater than 3°F.	out of position, reposition or replace.
2. Incorrect refrigerant pump discharge pressure	- pump pressure; should be approximately 4 PSIG.	Inspect evaporator spray nozzles. Clean if necessary.
	- Refrigerant charge.	Add refrigerant at full load until overflow temperature begins to drop.
	- refrigerant pump impeller.	If worn, replace.
	- pump rotation, should be counter-clockwise as viewed from the pump end.	If incorrect reverse motor rotation.

TROUBLE: WEAK SOLUTION IN ABSORBER, UNABLE TO CONCENTRATE WITH STEAM VALVE WIDE OPEN AT FULL LOAD.—Continued.

CAUSE	CHECK	CORRECTION
1. Vapor condensate above 110°F	- condensing water approach, leaving condenser water temperature to vapor condensate temperature should not be greater than 8°F.	Clean condenser tubes.
	- condensing sea water flow	Clean inlet sea water strainer - adjust condenser bypass valve.
	- refrigerant overflow temperature	If below 45°F, remove refrigerant until temperature begins to rise.
	- calibration of vapor condensate thermometer	recalibrate
2. Strong solution Temperature below 205°F.	- steam pressure	Raise steam pressure to 18 PSIG at generator inlet.
	- steam strainer	Clean strainer
	- steam traps	Open bypass valve, if any change is noted in solution temperature, repair traps.

REFRIGERATION AND AIR CONDITIONING

TROUBLE CHART FOR ABSORPTION TYPE (LITHIUM-BROMIDE) REFRIGERATION SYSTEM—Continued.

TROUBLE: SOLIDIFICATION DURING OPERATION—Continued

CAUSE	CHECK	CORRECTION
3. Low solution flow to generator	- calibration of strong solution thermometer - generator pump discharge pressure. Should be 4 PSIG, approximately.	Recalibrate Inspect valves for restrictions. Inspect generator spray nozzles. Clean or replace.

TROUBLE: SOLIDIFICATION DURING OPERATION

CAUSE	CHECK	CORRECTION
1. See over concentration of solution in absorber.		
2. See poor evaporator performance.		Desolidify machine
3. Sudden drop in entering condensing sea water temperature.	- 3-way pneumatic mixing valve (4) and condensing water temperature control.	Correct reason for malfunction of valve or control.
4. Sudden rise in steam pressure above 18 PSIG.	- control air pressure to steam control pilot and steam regulating valve bypass (12).	Reduce control air pressure to 15 PSIG and make certain valve is closed.

TROUBLE: LOST SOLUTION LEVEL IN ABSORBER

CAUSE	CHECK	CORRECTION
1. Heat exchanger strong solution valve restricted	- valve closed or collapsed diaphragm	Open valve. Replace diaphragm.

TROUBLE: PURGE WILL NOT OPERATE

CAUSE	CHECK	CORRECTION
1. Off on safety	- solution level in purge tank	Drain solution from tank. Clean probes.
2. Malfunction of purge pump.	- purge pump starter - purge level control - purge pressurestat - purge pump motor	Repair or replace if necessary.

TROUBLE: LOSS OF VACUUM DURING SHUT DOWN PERIOD

CAUSE	CHECK	CORRECTION
1. Valve open.	- all of these valves	Close valves and pull vacuum on machine.

TERMINOLOGY AND TROUBLESHOOTING

TROUBLE CHART FOR ABSORPTION TYPE (LITHIUM-BROMIDE) REFRIGERATION SYSTEM—Continued.

TROUBLE: LOSS OF VACUUM DURING SHUT-DOWN PERIOD. —Continued.

	CAUSE	CHECK	CORRECTION
2.	Pneumatic purge valve stuck open.	- purge valve operation air pressure to valve diaphragm	Repair if necessary. Open air bleed or correct reason for purge EP relay not closing and bleeding air.
3.	Seal leak	- water level in seal water tank, should be above suction and connection of seal water pump.	Replace leaking seal
4.	Check valve in seal water make up line did not seat	- ball check and check valve seat.	Replace ball check or repair valve seat.
5.	Leak in machine proper	- leak test machine.	Repair all leaks

TROUBLE: LOSS OF VACUUM DURING OPERATION

	CAUSE	CHECK	CORRECTION
1.	Seal leak	- all pump seals	Replace faulty seal.
2.	Malfunction of purge pump	- purge pump starter - purge pump motor	Repair if necessary Replace if burned out.

TROUBLE: REFRIGERANT OVERFLOW TEMPERATURE ALWAYS COLD MUST REMOVE REFRIGERANT PERIODICALLY

	CAUSE	CHECK	CORRECTION
1.	Tube leak.	- leak test across all tube bundles.	-Repair any leaks.
2.	Purge cooling coil.	- level in purge tank for an extended period while purge pump is off.	-Repair leaky coil if level in tank rises during test.

TROUBLE: COPPER PLATING

	CAUSE	CHECK	CORRECTION
1.	Air leakage into machine.	- leak test.	-Repair any leaks.
2.	Did not break vacuum with nitrogen and provide continuous bleed during repair work.	- procedure for breaking vacuum with nitrogen.	

REFRIGERATION AND AIR CONDITIONING

TROUBLE CHART FOR ABSORPTION TYPE (LITHIUM-BROMIDE) REFRIGERATION SYSTEM—Continued.

TROUBLE: MACHINE SHUT DOWN ON SAFETY

CAUSE	CHECK	CORRECTION
1. Power failure and control failure.	- fuses and power supply.	-Replace blown fuses and restore power.
2. Shutdown on low temperature cutout switch.	- switch setting.	-Set at 36°F.
	- chilled water temperature and steam valve.	-Recalibrate control and adjust steam valve.
3. Shutdown on chilled water failure switch.	- switch setting	-Set at 360 GPM minimum.
	- chilled water pump operation.	-Start pump.
	- chilled water flow.	-Open chilled water line valves.
4. Sea water pump, chilled water pump, refrigerant pump, or absorber-generator pump motor trips out on overload.	- heater elements.	-Install correct size.
	- amperage draw of motor.	-Find reason for overload if present.
	- power supply to all phases.	-Should be 440-3-60AC.
	- ambient temperature around starter too high.	-Provide air circulation or move starter.
	- pump head against pump curves.	-Correct reason for abnormal pump head.
	- binding due to impeller or bearing wear.	-Change impeller or bearings.
	- solidification in absorber-generator pump.	-Desolidify.

HVAC TERMS

Basic Cooling Circuit
Basic cooling is heat-moving - heat absorption. Heat is absorbed when liquid is boiled to a vapor. The temperature at which liquid boils is determined by pressure. Reducing pressure lowers the boiling point, and increasing pressure raises the boiling point. Water boils at 212°F at sea level; higher altitude lowers the boiling point. Boilers use the principle of heating water under pressure to raise the boiling point.

Simple Cooling Circuit = enclosed chamber (evaporator), compressor, expansion device, metering device, discharge device, filter-drier sight glass

Compressor

Maintains low pressure - reduces pressure on vapor on intake stroke, compresses vapor on compression stroke, discharges vapor under high pressure at outlet.

Compressors = Reciprocating piston driven by internally sealed motor or shaft driven by external (open-drive) motor. Hermetically sealed/welded housing; semi-hermetically bolted housing. Seal on the open drive is a disadvantage; it may leak. Small appliance compressors are often the rotary type, hermetically sealed. Residential A/C, refrigeration, hermetic/semi-hermetic rec. piston or scroll type. Large compressors (chillers, cooling plants) rec./screw/centrifugal type. Must cool compressor motor.

Expansion Device = expansion valve, capillary tube, fixed restrictor. Small, easily clogged orifices.

Low Side = metering device, evaporator, expansion device, and intake (suction) side of compressor. Accumulator traps liquid at outlet of evaporator. Low side pressures are typically under 100 psi.

High Side = discharge side of compressor, condenser and liquid line. Receivers to store excess refrigerant at outlet of condenser.

Filter-Drier

Filters contaminants, removes moisture. Sight glass in liquid line to view flow. Indicator of proper charge is solid liquid flowing through sight glass.

Condenser

High pressure heat transfer coil; accepts high temperature-high pressure gas from compressor, cools and condenses it to a low temperature-high pressure liquid.

Refrigerant

Liquid with a boiling point below desired evaporator temperature. For A/C refrigerants a boiling point below 70° F.

Access = pinched-off tubes (small), Schrader valves (medium), service valves (large, 3 positions)

Relief valves = protect against excessive high pressure. Relief valves cannot be installed in series. Test pressures cannot exceed rating on dataplate.

Superheated gas ideal for compressors (no liquid).

Compressor Lubricants
Long list of requirements. High miscibility (ability to mix with refrigerants). Polyester or "ester" based lubricants. Use alkylbenzenes for ternary blends containing HCFC's. Generally never mix lubricants.

Leak Detection
System must be sealed for reliability and environment.

Vacuum Pump
System must be evacuated and dehydrated prior to charging. Contaminants change pressure/temperature relationship and will cause system failure. Acids produced will corrode metal parts, decrease performance, and increase service needs.

Evacuation Procedure
Pressure Readings = relative to a pressure zone.
Absolute Pressure = outer space, total vacuum, zero pressure (0 psi Absolute)
Gauge Pressure = pressure relative to atmospheric pressure of 14.7 psi.
A gauge calibrated to read absolute pressure reads 14.7 *psia.* When disconnected at sea level, it reads 0 psia in deep space. A gauge calibrated to read gauge pressure reads 0 *psig* when disconnected at sea level and -14.7 psig in space. Gauge readings are more useful in A/C-Refrigeration. Temperature/pressure charts generally use gauge and Fahrenheit values.
Inches of Mercury (in Hg) are used for pressures below atmospheric; always gauge readings.
Microns of Mercury = 500 micron vacuum is adequate for more refrigerant circuit evacuations.

Manifold Gauge Set
Used for preliminary leak checking, evacuation, charging and refrigerant transfer.
Consists of a pair of gauges and a manifold chamber.
Low pressure gauge on left and blue; high pressure gauge on right and red.
Three sections of manifold chamber: Low side (left), high side (right) and center hose flow control.
Center service hose connected to external equipment needed for specific job (evacuation, charging, recovery, etc.)
Opening hand valve opens chamber to pressure of center chamber. Both valves open all three chambers at same pressure.

www.ingramcontent.com/pod-product-compliance
Lightning Source LLC
Chambersburg PA
CBHW081822300426
44116CB00014B/2447